To Harold and Dorothy

perhaps one day our dream

will come true.

and we'll sail the Aegean blue.

with best wishes for your

christmas 1978.

from Peter & Lucy.

BYRON'S GREECE

A  BOOK

Elizabeth Longford

BYRON'S GREECE

PHOTOGRAPHS BY
Jorge Lewinski

HARPER & ROW, PUBLISHERS

New York, Evanston, San Francisco, London

In memory of
Dennis Walwin Jones MC
Chairman of the Byron Society

CONTENTS

ΒΡΕΤΤΑΝΙΗΣ ΟΜΟΤΙΜΟΝ ΑΘΡΕΙ ΣΤΑΣ ΞΕΙΝΕ ΒΥΡΩΝΑ
ΟΝ ΠΕΡΙ ΚΗΡΙ ΦΙΛΕΥΝ ΜΝΗΜΟΣΥΝΗΣ ΘΥΓΑΤΡΕΣ
ΤΩΝ Δ ΕΥΕΡΓΕΩΝ ΜΝΗΣΤΙΝ ΣΩΙΖΟΝΤΕΣ ΑΓΗΡΩ
ΕΛΛΗΝΕΣ ΣΤΗΣΑΝ ΛΑΙΝΟΝ ΕΞ ΕΡΑΝΟΥ
ΕΥΤΕ ΓΑΡ ΕΛΛΑΣ ΕΤΕΙΡΕΤ ΕΛΕΥΘΕΡΙΗΣ ΕΝ ΑΕΘΛΩΙ
ΗΛΥΘΕ ΘΑΛΠΩΡΗ ΧΑΡΜΑ ΤΕ ΜΑΡΝΑΜΕΝΟΙΣ

INTRODUCTION

Byron belongs to Greece. 'But he is not your Lord Byron, he is *our* Lord Byron' protested the Mayor of Missolonghi, in the autumn of 1973. He had been asked to join with the British Byron Society in celebrating the forthcoming 150th anniversary of the poet's death on 19 April 1824. Of course the people of Missolonghi would be only too pleased to cooperate in the wreath-laying – on the understanding that he was *their* Lord Byron.

A wreath-laying ceremony duly took place on 1 May 1974. There had been a sudden sharp clap of thunder and a flash of lightning in the middle of the night before, as if in remembrance of the storm which raged during Byron's dying hours. But not a drop of rain fell. The crowd which gathered around the Byron Monument in the memorial garden next morning were moved and surprised, Greeks and foreigners alike, to find how much had been achieved by the citizens in honour of '*their* Byron', since the garden was planted after the destruction of his house. Most of the old iron railings had been removed and the knee-high grass and weeds which sadden so many monuments the world over, swept away. In their place an open square was laid out with low white walls, benches, and English garden flowers: marigolds, sweet williams and roses.

The solemn Greek prayers of thanksgiving for Byron's life and death were followed by the ringing oration of a young, liberal-minded schoolteacher, who recalled the coming to Missolonghi of 'the Man from the North' – with unimagined consequences to freedom throughout Greece. The theme of the response from the people of 'the North' was taken from the Gospel of St John: 'Greater love has no man than this, that he lay down his life for his friends.'

After Shakespeare, Byron is above all the British poet whose name arouses strong possessive instincts elsewhere. Germany, France, Italy, Russia – none of them fails to detect the accents of Byron in their own poetry and literature, or to see his image reflected in their painting and music. Nor is Byron forgotten in North and South America. He has a special place in the New World, for he thought more than once of emigrating to the United States or Bolivia.

It was said in Athens during a memorial lecture of 1974 that two men had conquered the world last century: Napoleon and Byron. One ruled men's bodies, the other their minds. If Byron were alive today he would be far from displeased to find himself thus associated with Bonaparte; but he would be

The statue of Byron in the Garden of Heroes, Missolonghi.

even happier to know that the place he had won in Greek hearts was still secure.

If Greece did not give him birth, it was unquestionably the country which gave birth to all that we mean by 'Byronic' in his poetry. As he himself said: 'If I am a poet it is the air of Greece which has made me one.' If he met his death in Greece, he also found there the springs of an extraordinary, unlooked-for immortality.

A word on the spelling of proper names is necessary. Naturally Byron's own spelling appears in all quotations, though he himself admitted that orthography was not his strong point, writing in *Don Juan*:

> *The Kozacks, or, if so you please, Cossacques –*
> *(I don't much pique myself upon orthography,*
> *So that I do not grossly err in facts,*
> *Statistics, tactics, politics, and geography) –*

Byron's geography was unimpeachable, but there was an added complication in Greek place-names. The town of Ioannina, for instance, was spelt thus by Byron's travelling companion Hobhouse, but Byron wrote it Yanina, while today it can also be written Jannina. Where names have changed radically in the course of centuries I have mentioned other versions.

Greece is the focal point of this story, both in text and pictures. Therefore the years which the poet spent in England, Italy or elsewhere outside Greece have been treated only in short, linking pieces. This has necessitated the barest mention of such controversial issues as his relations with Caroline Lamb, Augusta Leigh, Annabella Milbanke, Claire Clairmont and Allegra, with the result that just criticisms may seem to have been glossed over. Certainly this has not been my intention; any more than it would be my wish that those episodes should cast unfair shadows over the Greek story.

I would like to conclude these words of introduction with warm thanks to the Byron Society for the generous help many of their members have given me; and for the pleasure of the company of those who went to Greece for the Byron celebrations of April and May 1974. Jorge Lewinski's evocative pictures and the notes for my text were made during the celebrations. As members of the Byron Society we travelled over much of Greece and were privileged to join with many Greek cities, towns and villages in their commemorative events.

Finally I think back with gratitude to Oxford, where I first studied the Greek language and history; and with nostalgia to the Greece I first saw through the eyes of Sir Maurice Bowra, Sir Mortimer Wheeler and Gervase Mathew, all inspired lecturers. Sir Maurice once ended a book with the ringing words, 'They were the Greeks.' I shall add, 'He was Byron.'

Part I

CHILDE HAROLD'S PILGRIMAGE

1 Youth: 'Hazard and Burgundy'

George Gordon, 6th Lord Byron, was born in rented lodgings at 16 Holles Street, London, on 22 January 1788. His mother could not afford to stay long in the capital. She had married a debonair playboy who, having swiftly squandered her substantial fortune, only visited her when the coast was clear of bailiffs. He was more interested in her presenting him with an occasional remittance than with a son and heir.

Captain John ('Mad Jack') Byron, George Byron's father, was the son of Admiral John ('Foulweather Jack') Byron and of Sophia Trevanion of Cornwall, his cousin. The captain's uncle was the 5th Lord Byron, a 'Wicked Lord' according to local legend, because of his prowess with housemaids and a drunken duel in which he killed one of his cronies. Meanwhile Captain John Byron had become a consummate lady-killer. Nine years before George's birth he eloped with an heiress who was already the wife of Lord Carmarthen. After a divorce they were married, and she bore him one daughter, Augusta Mary Byron, the poet's half-sister. Not long afterwards Augusta's mother died. Hardly had 'Mad Jack' gone through his first wife's fortune before he found, and ruined, a second heiress and wife, Byron's mother, Catherine Gordon of Gight in Aberdeenshire.

Like so many Byrons – and incidentally Trevanions also – the captain loved a woman of his own family. This was his sister, Frances Leigh, wife of General Leigh. Their son, Colonel Leigh, was to marry his cousin Augusta Mary Byron. There is no doubt that 'Mad Jack's' affection for his sister Mrs Leigh was incestuous; nor that his son George Gordon Byron inherited all three of his father's predelictions: compulsive spending, womanising and incest. Catherine Byron's stepdaughter Augusta was to become the second Mrs Leigh of whom a Byron was over-fond.

Byron's mother contributed to his make-up a healthy Scottish money sense. Overlaid though it was in his 'hot youth' by the spendthrift genes on his father's side, this maternal gift of carefulness returned to Byron in his thirties, to the great advantage of himself, his relatives and his Cause – Greece. Unfortunately Catherine Gordon also passed on to her son a stormy temperament, together with physical corpulence. In due course Byron learned to control his own tendency to plumpness, and to allow his rages only the briefest possible eruptions. From his mother he may also have inherited a romantic attachment to the ancient nobility. She boasted of royal Stuart descent through a daughter of King James I of Scotland who married a Gordon. The Byrons claimed Norman blood.

If Byron's story owes much to the hidden and overt persuasions of his parentage, it owes no less to his lameness. His right foot and ankle were distorted from birth. At three his walking was still ungainly, like a much younger child. That was the year when his father died in France. 'I perfectly remember him', Byron said years afterwards, 'and had a very early horror of matrimony, from the sight of domestic broils. . . .'

Since he was a year old George Gordon Byron had been settled with his mother in Aberdeen, where they continued to live until he was ten. Catherine Byron cleverly scraped along on the remaining £150 income from her marriage settlement. Young Geordie went to Aberdeen Grammar School at six, where his 'devil' of a temper matched Mama's outbursts at home. He remembered her as always 'thundering against Somebody or other' – often against him.

His nurse Agnes Gray had given him a genuine love of the Psalms and a harsh grounding in Calvinism. Yet the prospective torments of Calvin's hell were as nothing to his ever-present lame foot. Proud and sensitive, the handicapped child was not helped by his mother's tauntings. 'Lame brat', she would call him; and all her spoilings of him between whiles, not to mention her sacrifices and scrimping for his sake, could not compensate for his humiliation.

Newstead Abbey in 1832, engraved by Lindin after Westall.

Even so, there were romantic times during his Scottish period. He was in love at eight with his little cousin Mary Duff, and in love more permanently with the rivers and mountains of Deeside. The steep slopes of Loch-Na-Gar (the subject also of Queen Victoria's rhapsodies) stuck in his memory, to be recalled when he first saw the mountains of Greece.

At ten years old the bell of destiny rang for the shy but likeable young Scot, who spoke with a burr, called himself a 'laddie', and was known as 'Mrs Byron's crookit deevil'. His great-uncle, the 'Wicked' 5th Lord Byron, died. Geordie was the heir. In August he and his mother went south, to take up residence under the baronial but leaky roof of Newstead Abbey in Notting-hamshire. The place was hopelessly encumbered with debt and dilapidated. But to the ten-year-old boy it was romance incarnate. King Henry VIII had rewarded an earlier Byron with the lands of Newstead at the dissolution of the monasteries. There was still a ghost in 1798 when the young 6th Lord arrived. A waterfall, lakes and mock forts in the approved eighteenth-century fashion were set off by the magnificent façade of the old Abbey, with its tall traceried windows lending the distinction of their ruined gothic beauty to the adjacent mansion.

Thanks to the lame foot, however, he was torn away from Newstead the next year, 1799, and confined in an uncompromising square brick house in Nottingham, next door to the Infirmary. A notable quack from the Infirm-ary squeezed his foot to no avail in agonising splints. At night his nurse May Gray, sister of Agnes, after drinking around the town would roll into her young charge's bed and introduce him to sex. Disgusted, he complained to his lawyer. May Gray was sacked and the young lord whisked to London, where he attended a boarding school in Dulwich.

In April 1801 he entered Harrow School. Already a powerful swimmer, he succeeded in playing cricket for Harrow against Eton. Though another boy had to run for him, and though his team was 'most confoundedly beat', he was justifiably proud of a genuine athleticism achieved by will-power. At Harrow he studied the classics, with happy results when he visited the land of Leonidas and Sappho. His classical expertise also enabled him to con-verse in lewd shorthand with male friends, through the mediation of Petronius.

There were no untoward sexual adventures for Byron at school, but plenty of romantic attachments to young favourites. These experiences may have helped to nurture a youthful melancholy. He would often recall the hours spent musing under his favourite elm tree at Harrow-on-the-Hill. As he reclined on a grave-stone, he could look across to distant Windsor. Many years later, he was to recline on a group of flat rocks, but below him would be fields of olives and the Ionian Sea. And his melancholy would have its roots in the real political trials and tribulations of Greek politics, not in mere *weltschmerz*.

During his Harrow days Byron's experience of sex was expanded in the holidays. Newstead had had to be let. Its tenant was Lord Grey de Ruthyn, a young nobleman who flirted with Mrs Byron and made advances to her son. Though Byron recoiled in horror, it is possible to see how a boy of his temperament, in whom feelings of attraction and repulsion were always close together, would return in the East to practices which had revolted him in England, but which out there had been long sanctioned by life and literature.

Byron was in fact passionately in love with a beautiful neighbour and cousin, Mary Chaworth of Annesley Hall. Byron's mother had taken Burgage Manor on the green at Southwell. Her son had nothing to amuse him except chat with the friendly Pigot family across the road. In August 1803 he temporarily escaped from Southwell ('this horrid place . . . no society but old parsons and old Maids. . . .') by lodging in the Newstead gate-house. Here he trained himself to be an expert shot, and some of his practice shots can still be seen in the wooden gate of nearby Annesley Hall. Mary Chaworth was engaged to a Colonel Musters. That autumn Byron was too unhappy to return to Harrow and his mother allowed him to miss a whole term. He was now only just sixteen. His three, very different experiences with May Gray, Lord Grey and Mary Chaworth explain his already cynical attitude towards sex, not least when associated with matrimony. Writing at seventeen to Augusta, he proposed to enjoy a long period of bachelor freedom before making himself 'miserable with matrimonial clog'.

In October 1805 Byron entered a place which he was to describe as 'a villainous Chaos of Dice and Drunkenness, nothing but Hazard and Burgundy, Hunting, mathematics, and Newmarket, Riot and Racing. . . .' This was Trinity College, Cambridge. All the same, it was 'a Paradise compared with the eternal dullness of Southwell, oh ! the misery of doing nothing, but make *Love, enemies,* and *Verses.*' But if he had made juvenile verses and had them privately printed at Southwell, at Cambridge he was to make a book – and get it published. His *Hours of Idleness* appeared in June 1807. At Cambridge, moreover, he showed his true mettle in a choice of remarkable friends.

One was a brilliant scoffer, another a classical star and mischievous gambler, a third was soaked in literature and religion, a fourth – the devoted John Cam Hobhouse – was absorbed by history and politics. All were distinguished for their scholarship, wit, and for their love of Byron.

There was also the moment in Trinity College chapel when he first laid eyes on the chorister, John Edleston, and heard his voice.

And like music on the waters
Is thy sweet voice to me.

He loved Edleston with a deep, protective love, went walks with him every day, and gave him money. These years he called 'the most romantic period of my life', and his experience was that of 'a violent though *pure*, love and passion'.

By the beginning of 1806 he was desperately in debt. Though still a minor, he was introduced to the money-lenders who enabled him to finance his London dissipations. These easily eclipsed his exploits at Cambridge and centred around 'Vice, Riots, Balls & Boxing matches, Dowagers & demi-reps, Cards & Crim-con [divorce proceedings], ... Love & Lotteries, Brookes's [Club] & Bonaparte, Exhibitions of pictures with Drapery, & *women without*. ... Opera-singers & Orators, Wine, Women, Wax works, & Weather cocks. ...' Greatest of all weathercocks was the young Lord himself, who at this date confessed his disposition to be '(in general) change-able'.

He went down from Cambridge at Christmas 1807 owing thousands of pounds. But there was another set of figures which reflected on him nothing but credit. At the age of nineteen he had resolved with characteristic firmness to control his weight. He reduced it in six months from 14 stone 6 lbs (at only (5 feet 7½ ins tall) to 10 stone 11 lbs by wearing seven waistcoats and a great-coat, hot baths, no breakfast, no supper, no beer, hardly any meat, and doses of physic. No wonder his clothes were taken in *'half a yard'*. But the human form which was thus abused at least regained its pristine Greek beauty. There were few women who would not risk a 'crim-con' for those dark curls with a chestnut glint, the pale, dreaming forehead and the lips which would not have shamed the Apollo Belvedere – a classical statue recently seized by Napoleon Bonaparte from the Vatican and exhibited in the Louvre.

Lord Byron was accused of being addicted to 'low company'. Certainly he liked unusual company. He kept a tame bear at Cambridge whom he was said to embrace like a brother. The bear 'should *sit* for *a Fellowship*', declared his master, when asked what he intended to do with him. Here was more than an echo of Caligula creating his horse a consul. Bruin, however, after hugging a 'little' Cambridge man too enthusiastically, was sent to Newstead without his MA. Byron had reoccupied Newstead in September 1808. He and his Cambridge friends celebrated with suitable orgies in which they would stagger about the Abbey dressed up as monks. At Newstead Byron's inseparable companion had been his black-and-white Newfoundland dog, Boatswain; but Boatswain died that November and was buried in the garden beneath a substantial monument inscribed by his master with, what some considered, excessive poetic licence:

> *To mark a Friend's remains these stones arise;*
> *I knew but one unchanged – and here he lies.*

Byron felt at this dreary moment that the animal world was closer to him than man. He described himself as 'a friendless animal'.

He acquired a new 'friend' about Christmas time. (Hobhouse had been staying but had gone home and Byron was lonely.) It was the skull of 'some jolly friar' dug up at Newstead. Death was a favourite ingredient of the Romantic movement, and Byron had his lugubrious new accomplice made into a drinking cup. The skull-cup, he wrote in a satiric poem, was the only head from which 'Whatever flows is never dull'. Life at Newstead had become as empty as the skull and much duller. He had fathered an illegitimate son on a housemaid; he had dined with Mary Chaworth, now Mrs Musters, at Annesley Hall, a devastating experience; he had completed a biting satire called *English Bards and Scotch Reviewers*, in which he lashed the *Edinburgh Review* for ridiculing his own *Hours of Idleness*; he had taken his seat in the House of Lords, looking rather paler than usual, on 13 March 1809, for he had ceased to be a minor and became twenty-one years old that January. Now he was bankrupt but free.

He had only one ambition, to go East. Like death, the East was infinitely fascinating to the romantic spirit. Nothing now held him in England but lack of means to travel. Ignoring his mountain of debt which had risen to £13,000, he ordered his agent to raise money for his travels by selling off an estate he owned in Rochdale. Unluckily, however, this valuable property turned out to be virtually unsaleable owing to the dubious financial operations of his great-uncle, the 'Wicked Lord'.

Nevertheless, Byron's need to travel was imperious and absolute. It was recognised as such by his friends, and one of them, after a sumptuous gambling *coup*, lent him over £4,000. Byron in turn promised a loan to his chosen companion for the journey, John Cam Hobhouse, whose eagerness to travel and general pennilessness matched Byron's own. The two pilgrims sailed from Falmouth on 2 July 1809, both outwardly as jolly as the friars whom Byron had pictured at Newstead three centuries before. Beneath the surface, however, Byron was still gloomy. He had told his agent there was a secret reason for his leaving England. It may have been increasingly physical love for or from Edleston. Travelling by way of Lisbon and Malta, they would make for the Isles of Greece – those 'Edens of the Eastern wave'.

2   Greece: His Greenest Island

Byron's moodiness vanished with his first glimpse of Portugal. He fell in love with the mountain village of Cintra, writing to his mother that it was 'perhaps in every respect, the most delightful in Europe. . . .' Within three months, the Greek village of Zitza was challenging even 'Cintra's glorious Eden' in Byron's estimation, while in six months' time the Attic plain was to beat all. But so far, Portugal was queen: 'I loves oranges, and talks bad latin to the monks', he wrote to a Cambridge friend, '. . . and I swims in the Tagus all across at once. . . .' Like the young in every age he camouflaged his emotion with mocking language.

There were even more oranges and women no less golden when they arrived in Seville, doing their seventy miles a day on horseback. Byron left Seville loaded with a stupendous tress of lady's hair. At Cádiz the women's beauty merited a poetic tribute:

> *Oh never talk again to me*
> > *Of northern climes and British ladies;*
> *It has not been your lot to see,*
> > *Like me, the lovely Girl of Cadiz.*

Byron hated making word pictures of scenery – 'damn description, it is always disgusting' – but a pretty woman went naturally into verse. Little did he guess that the Girl of Cádiz was soon to be superseded by the Maid of Athens.

Meanwhile, there were still two more emotional hoops to go through before he reached Greece.

From Gibraltar he sent home his good-looking young page, Robert Rushton, a Newstead boy and great favourite with his master. 'Turkey is in too dangerous a state for boys to enter', he explained to his agent. Greece of course was merely a province of the Turkish Empire, the Greek War of Independence being still some years distant.

Having parted from Robert, Byron spent the voyage from Gibraltar to Malta in sad, solitary musing, except when a chance came for pistol-shooting (at empty bottles on deck), a sport which he always considered highly agree-able and useful in those violent times. Otherwise he would sit for hours in the shrouds, 'enamoured, it may be', as a fellow-traveller speculated, 'of the moon'. Of Robert Rushton, more likely.

Malta provided him with a passionate love-affair. The girl was Constance Spencer Smith, wife of the British Minister at Stuttgart (and British Consul in Malta) and daughter of the Austrian Ambassador. At last, on 19 Septem-ber, he and Hobhouse embarked in the brig *Spider* for the Ionian Sea. Byron still had with him a living reminder of Newstead and English ways – his valet Fletcher. This uncompromisingly insular servant was to see Byron through the whole of his brief life's pilgrimage; such was Fletcher's devotion to his lord.

Rising out of a calm autumnal sea the mountains of Greece first became visible on 23 September. It was the Greek mainland, known then as the Morea and now as the Peloponnese. As you sail between the Ionian islands of Cephalonia and Zante into the Gulf of Patras, the peaks along the shore take on strange shapes: sometimes like Olympian goddesses with streaming hair and heaving breasts, at others like monsters with a succession of humps

Byron's first sight of the Greek mainland: the mountains guarding the approach to Missolonghi.

16

or sharp combs. Three days after sighting them, Byron and Hobhouse were landed at Patras, in a currant ground. There and then they celebrated their arrival on Greek soil by a session of pistol-shooting.

They were looked after for the day by the British Consul, Mr Strané, 'a good kind man very ugly', as Hobhouse called him. Some of the outstanding buildings of Patras appeared much the same in 1809 as they do now: the arcaded streets; the long mole; the huge castle with its brown inner and outer walls and battlemented towers, perhaps even its locust on the footpath, today clearly containing the transmigrated soul of the Turkish governor. We can still see sheds along the quay prominently marked with the word 'Currants'. The 'Domestica' wine is dry and pleasant and not too resinous. No doubt the two pilgrims of 1809 assessed it, although they arrived and departed on the same day.

Sailing up the west coast of Greece towards Prevesa, they passed between Rion (the Castle of the Morea) and Antirrion (the Castle of Roumeli) in the Gulf of Patras, the latter with its typical squat, dun Turkish fort, and the mighty range of Parnassus in the distance. On their left lay Ithaca, the island home of Odysseus, floating on the blue sea like a pair of water-wings with its two great hills and narrow isthmus joining them. A few windmills were visible by day and shepherds' fires by night. Byron was moved by 'the barren spot on Ithaca' where 'sad Penelope' sat looking out to sea for the return of her husband; but more deeply moved by the 'far-projecting' rock of Leucadia (Levkas) from which the broken-hearted Lesbian, Sappho, flung herself to death. The evening star shining over this most melancholy scene calmed and soothed him.

He had felt no premonitory shudder at seeing the town of Missolonghi (Messolongion) to his right. Yet on this day in Greece, his very first, he was in fact observing the scene of his last.

By the 28th they had reached the small port of Prevesa. They spent the night on board, watching a romantic moonrise over the bay of Actium. Nothing could be more beautiful by night or by day than this historic region, the bay open at one end to the Ionian Sea, and at the other forming part of the much larger Ambracian Gulf. The waters of the Gulf are encircled by distant blue mountains and dotted with innumerable islets, its shores scolloped with green coves, its smooth surfaces broken by strange white threads of foam or dark currents. There is more green pasture here than in most of Western Greece. Pairs of white horses as well as oxen can be seen ploughing, and an occasional small herd of cows grazing, instead of only tough, resilient goats.

Actium itself seems to have been designed as a haunt of ancient peace. Everyone notices, just as Byron did, the surprising contrast between the miniature bay and the great event which took place there. When he revisited Actium on his way south again he wrote to his mother: 'Today I saw the

Ruins of the city of Nicopolis built by Augustus in celebration of his victory at the Battle of Actium.

The bay of Actium, where
Byron anchored for the
night of 28 September
1809 before landing
at Prevesa.

remains of the town of *Actium* near which Anthony lost the world in a small bay where two frigates could hardly manoeuvre, a broken wall is the sole remnant.' Augustus defeated Anthony and Cleopatra in a naval battle, thus changing the civilised world. It is perhaps equally surprising that Byron's first sight of Actium did not inspire him to write a tragic sonnet. That task was left to the French *fin de siècle* poet, José-Maria de Heredia, who imagined Mark Anthony bending over Cleopatra and suddenly seeing, reflected in her huge eyes, as on a wine-dark ocean, his fleeing galleys: *Toute une mer immense où fuyaient des galères.* The truth was that Byron's meditations on Actium were never portentous. The idea of a man making war, and throwing away all the kingdoms of the earth for a woman, was presented by him either as perfectly natural or faintly funny. That second vision of Actium on his way back from the north inspired him with a love lyric, as we shall see. But in *Childe Harold* he expressed only the irony of the situation:

> *Ambracia's gulf behold, where once was lost*
> *A world for woman, lovely harmless thing!*

This was followed by a more irreverent mood when he emphasised the sick humour of war heroes 'and laughed at martial wight', having seen Actium, Lepanto and Trafalgar 'unmoved'. As for his much later *Don Juan*, here the sense of ridicule in his attitude to Anthony entirely prevails:

> *He died at fifty for a queen of forty. . . .*

Prevesa was not kind to Byron and Hobhouse on the day they ceremoniously landed, 30 September. A sudden deluge of rain soaked the scarlet military uniforms which they had brought with them to wear on all such formal occasions. (The British uniform would also help to over-awe bad characters.) The streets were little better than miry lanes, being unpaved, and the wretched huts of wood were thatched with over-hanging reeds which dripped down their necks. An immediate return to Patras was tempting. However, the handsome Greek who worked as the English Vice-Consul was good enough to put them up for the night; though he did not provide them with a privy which Byron could understand. Hobhouse describes in his diary how Byron, failing to negotiate the plank over the hole, sat on the hole 'with his knees to his nose'. Today Byron might fare better in the north-western mountains, where he would come across many porcelain structures with two white china 'feet' on either side. On these he would conveniently tread, like the page in the footsteps of good King Wenceslas.

From Prevesa the party set out between wide tussocky fields to view a spectacular Roman ruin. This was the remains of the mighty city of Nicopolis – Victory City – built by the Emperor Augustus to commemorate his victory over Anthony at the Battle of Actium. A few years before Byron arrived the Turks had been rooting about among the ruins to find materials for the

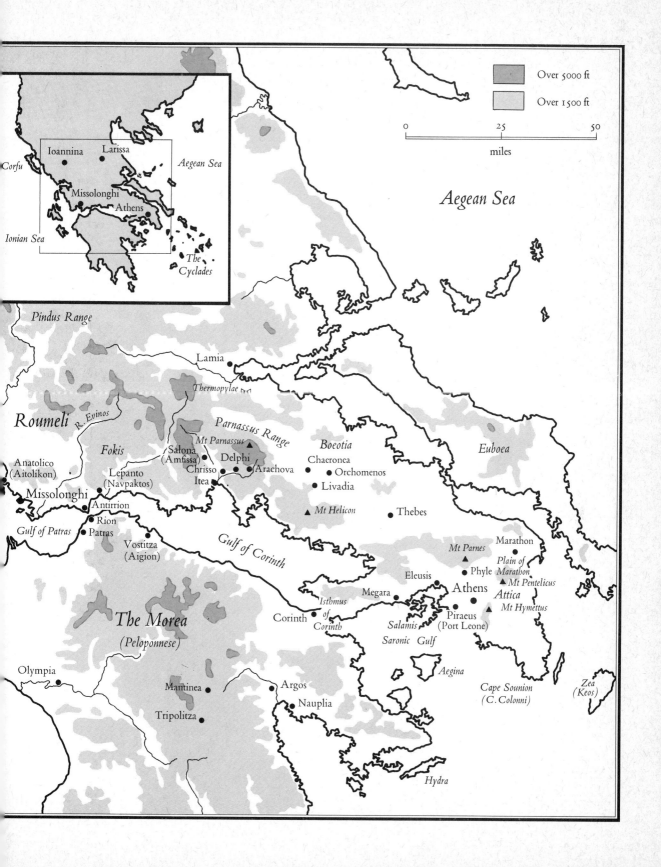

Over 5000 ft

Over 1500 ft

0   25   50

miles

Aegean Sea

Corfu

Ioannina

Larissa

Aegean Sea

Missolonghi

Athens

Ionian Sea

The Cyclades

Pindus Range

Lamia

Roumeli

R. Evinos

Thermopylae

Parnassus Range

Mt Parnassus ▲

Fokis

Salona (Amfissa)

Delphi

Boeotia

Chaeronea

Orchomenos

Euboea

Anatolico (Aitolikon)

Lepanto (Navpaktos)

Chrisso

Itea

Arachova

Livadia

Missolonghi

Antirrion

▲ Mt Helicon

Thebes

Rion

Patras

Gulf of Patras

Vostitza (Aigion)

Gulf of Corinth

Mt Parnes

Marathon

Plain of Marathon

Phyle

▲ Mt Pentelicus

Eleusis

Athens

Attica

The Morea

(Peloponnese)

Megara

Piraeus (Port Leone)

▲ Mt Hymettus

Isthmus of Corinth

Corinth

Salamis

Saronic Gulf

Olympia

Mantinea

Argos

Aegina

Cape Sounion (C. Colonni)

Zea (Keos)

Nauplia

Tripolitza

Hydra

Pasha's palace at Prevesa. But apparently the masonry was not up to the usual Roman standard. All the Pasha was able to use were inscriptions, which he put over the seraglio gate. One wonders what they were. Possibly a warning to other would-be Cleopatras.

There is little change in the general effect of Nicopolis since Byron's day. Victory City had itself been vanquished long ago by time and earthquake. When one sees the jagged segments of red-brick Roman walls with broken arches rising from the sheep-clipped turf, and beyond them, on the road northwards, a grey amphitheatre totally overgrown by grass and shrubs except for the outside circular wall, one can only agree with Byron that 'the second Caesar's trophies' are 'withering like the hand that reared them'. Or one can echo the memorable lines written by Byron's friend Shelley on another great ruin, that of Ozimandias, King of Kings, with its arrogant inscription:

Look on my works ye mighty and despair!

Byron did not much care for looking on the works of the classical past, however mighty. His was not the mind of the archaeologist, eager to perform acts of the minutest detection in order to reconstruct history. This was always Hobhouse's speciality. In the words of Edward John Trelawny, Byron's unreliable but perceptive friend: 'The Poet had an antipathy to everything scientific; maps and charts offended him; he would not look through a spy-glass ... buildings the most ancient or modern he was as indifferent to as he was to painting, sculpture, and music. [The last few words are typical of Trelawny's exaggeration.] But all natural objects and changes in the elements he was generally the first to point out and the last to lose sight of.'

If a ruin stirred Byron, it was more often to feelings of resentment than romance. Particularly did he deplore the desolation of a past which he loved as deeply as he loved classical Greece. At Nicopolis he was moved, indeed, but by the music of Greek sheep-bells between the cavernous Roman buildings, and the 'coax, coax' of Greek frogs in the ditches.

3   The Wild North-West

Back to Prevesa for the start on 1 October of their journey into the interior. Their immediate goal was the town of Ioannina, capital of the notorious potentate, Ali Pasha, who had extended his savage rule (nominally under the Sultan of Turkey in distant Constantinople) to include parts of Albania, Epirus (north-western Greece) and western Greece as far south as the Morea. Ioannina was famous for its lake, island and towering Mt Mitzikeli; its Turkish fortress, mosque and palace; its silversmiths, coppersmiths and other skilled workers in leather and wool. Epirus, of which Ioannina was the

The mountain range at Arta which Byron passed on his journey from Salora to Arta.

prosperous centre, sheltered in its fastness the wild but Christian Greek race of Suliots. With these brave people Byron was soon to become closely linked. And they would reappear dramatically in his life during the Greek War of Independence, when he returned in 1823 on a second and final 'pilgrimage', or rather 'crusade' to Greece.

There had to be one more short sea-trip from Prevesa before the cavalcade could take to the road. They were rowed by six boatmen to Salora on the Ambracian Gulf, the port for the historic town of Arta (formerly Ambracia),

The old Turkish pack-horse bridge at Arta.

where they would join the road north to Ioannina. They stayed two nights at Salora in a Turkish barrack, the second night held up by heavy rain. This visit afforded Byron his first convivial acquaintance with the local Albanian soldiery. He soon got used to the smoke from the long pipes and the weird songs, but not to the fashionable belching. Hobhouse was impressed by their 'strutting' walk – chests out and heads thrown back – and by their quiet curiosity about everything English. 'Pragmata Inglesika!' (English goods) they would remark, fingering the English watch-chains.

The next night's lodging, in the Greek customs-house of Arta, Hobhouse found very comfortable compared with Prevesa. 'Properly speaking', he grumbled, however, 'the word comfort could not be applied to anything I ever saw out of England.' They were kept awake by a party of Greeks dancing next door.

It is no longer necessary to bring one's own folding iron bedstead and mahogany travelling chest, mirror and dressing-table as Byron did, or to doss down with soldiers or officials. The Xenia hotels (meaning 'foreigner' or 'tourist') are good to sleep and eat in, and though an occasional handle falls off a window into a bath, cracking the new enamel, everything works, or is soon made to work. As for the roads, the side-roads can still be flooded in autumn and spring by torrential rains and mud, but a series of splendid mountain highways are almost completed. Groups of yellow diggers and tractors pulled up on the lay-bys show them for the magnificent feats of engineering they are.

Whether Byron and Hobhouse heard the legend of the ancient Turkish pack-horse bridge in Arta by which they entered and left the town, is not known. It was said that the stone-mason built his wife into the foundations in order to strengthen them. The travellers certainly did not realise that between Arta and Ioannina was one of the most famous classical centres in Greek history. The site of the Oracle of Dodona (now Dodone) lies within the jurisdiction of Arta. Here can still be seen the largest and oldest amphi-theatre in Greece lying in a green valley under the shadows of a bleak moun-tain. The oracle once boasted of 'Talking Oaks'. The rustling of these sacred ilex trees was believed to be the voice of the god Zeus, whose words the priests would interpret. Hobhouse had no idea that modern Dodone was so near, nor, when he and Byron later made an expedition from Ioannina to a magni-ficent but partially buried amphitheatre, that this was in fact part of the 'lost' shrine. Byron lamented in *Childe Harold*:

> *Oh! Where, Dodona! is thine aged grove,*
> *Prophetic fount and oracle divine?*

Byron's answer was a despairing, 'All, all forgotten'. Paradoxically, how-ever, the true answer was that much of the past had actually been lying under his own feet. Thanks to many successful 'digs', Dodone is now a great archaeological treasure-house in which the Greek citizenry, as well as visitors, take pride and interest. There are no longer oaks at Dodone. Other-wise almost all is remembered, contrary to Byron's fears. Perhaps one day there will be a civic move to replant the 'aged grove'. But it was not for loss of the sacred oaks that the Greek guide spoke nostalgically in Dodone 150 years after Byron's death. 'Here', he said wistfully, 'was our earliest Parliament.' Four months later Greece had a Parliament once more.

Leaving Arta, they passed through fields of rice and maize. The vintage was in full swing, and long strings of horses passed them loaded with goat-skins of new wine. Since the hairy side of the skins was turned inwards, the wine tasted strongly of goat. Later they climbed into rugged mountains, where they stared at the ferocious dogs and long guns of the shepherds, who in turn gazed back at their umbrellas.

The Byron cavalcade – ten horses carrying among other things four trunks and three beds, plus two Albanian soldiers to guard all this potential loot, the whole taking up a good deal more space than a coach-load of modern

The rugged mountains
near Arta through which
Byron and Hobhouse
travelled to Ioannina.

29

tourists – arrived in Ioannina on 5 October. It was a sparkling day. Boats, towers, domes, lake-waters and minarets lay all bright and glittering through the orange and lemon groves, not unlike early-morning London, as celebrated by Wordsworth on Westminster Bridge seven years earlier. Industrial development and the multi-storey buildings of a modern town today obscure the approach to Ioannina's beautiful Lake Pambotis. But from its banks or its surrounding hills it is unspoilt and seductive as ever. And there is no horror, such as sickened Byron and Hobhouse on entering the town: a man's torn side and arm – one of Ali Pasha's victims – hanging from a plane tree. As it was near a butcher's shop they thought at first that it was a piece of meat for sale.

Byron probably learned later from the British Resident, Captain William Martin Leake, that this was all that remained of a Greek patriot named Evtimio, who had planned a rising against the Turkish despot in the Ionian Islands with Russian help. He was captured, tortured for three months, executed on the day after Ali Pasha left the city for the north, 'and his four quarters hung upon the plane-trees at the entrance to Ioannina.'

In the silversmiths' street of the old town (Odhos Averoff) you can still see the sparks flying from the forges, and in the shop-windows embroiderers stitching or cobblers sitting cross-legged at their work. Within the castron or citadel (now called the Frourion), surrounded by its tremendous wall, minimally Byzantine mostly Turkish, the narrow streets huddle together. You can see the house where the lovely Greek girl, Kyra Frossyni (Lady Euphrosyne), lived before she and her fifteen or sixteen companions were allegedly raped by Ali and murdered. The story which Byron heard has several variants. Ali's great mosque has settled down into being a Greek national museum, while its tall slender minaret, no longer religiously ecstatic, is merely a useful though still somewhat dizzy view-point.

Outside the Frourion is Byron Street, a row of early-nineteenth-century stone houses with small, curved iron balconies to some of the first floor windows. A plaque on No. 3 says that Lord Byron lived in this *oichia* from 9 to 12 October 1809. *Oichia*, be it noted, means 'house' in Greek, not the site of a house. A Greek professor in nearby Metsovon insists that the poet lived in this very house, not merely in an older house on this site. And the Greek family who now live at No. 3 firmly believe the professor is right. They will invite you in, offer you a dish of candied pears, introduce you to their ninety-five-year-old grandmother and show you the long five-windowed front room with a balcony at each end, in which Byron lived. (Grandmothers seem to live to ninety-five in Ioannina. One of the same age occupies a spacious old Turkish house with an inner courtyard. Her granddaughter, another beautiful black-eyed Frossyni, entertains favoured visitors with ravishing pastries.) But Byron's biographer, the American professor, Leslie A. Marchand, will have none of No. 3. He has published the reproduction

Papyrus reeds fringe Lake Pambotis, near Ioannina.

30

of a print, dated 1820, (first published in the *Travels* of T. S. Hughes) which shows the original, wooden, Turkish-style house, with courtyard and outer staircase, where Byron lodged in Ioannina at the home of Signor Nicolo Argyri. The print exactly tallies with Captain Leake's description of Greeks' houses in Ioannina at that date. Was this, then, the original *oichia*, and is the present plaque inaccurate? The professors must fight it out, reaching a compromise settlement, one dares to hope, whereby it will be established that at least part of the older house remains in which Byron actually lived.

Metsovon is the picturesque village in the main pass of the Pindus range which best focuses the life and customs of these mountain peoples. Here the snow lies long. Among the distant rocks are still the lairs of wolves, wild boar and an occasional lynx – but no robbers. In Byron's day the village organised a permanent force of *armatoli* to combat robbers and keep the pass open. Golden eagles are no longer common but Pindus has its Egyptian and griffon vultures. The museum of Metsovon shows pottery, prints, silver work, rugs, cushions, kitchen utensils, clothing and best of all, the living habits of men and women in the days when Byron was a visitor. *Two* best bedrooms were necessary to the prosperous citizen: a summer bedroom, spacious and airy, a winter bedroom, tiny and cramped by the double bed, with oil lamps and no windows whatever. A few present-day citizens of Metsovon are conscious enough of their social history to go on wearing a traditional dress of a round black cap, short cloak and tunic, and long white woollen socks.

The poet's stay with Nicolo Argyri in Ioannina was greatly enhanced by the kind attentions of the British Resident, Captain Leake, who was later to write of Ali Pasha: 'It must be admitted that the success with which Aly has indulged his ambition in Greece and Albania, not only in defiance of the Porte [Ottoman government], but hitherto with a constant increase of influence ... is a proof of skill, foresight and constancy of purpose' – which the Pasha might have used for the good of his country. Instead, he was a 'criminal', ruling by force and fraud, patient only to deceive and interested in a civilised art, such as medicine, only to obtain love-potions and poisons. (*Travels in Northern Greece,* Vol. IV)

Ali himself was no less attentive than Leake to his English guests, courtesy to foreigners being Turkish good manners, and courtesy to the English being good policy. The old rascal happened to be staying at the time in his older capital of Tepelene, in Albania, where he was engaged in 'a little war' (*'une petite guerre'*) in Berat. Nevertheless, Ali saw to it that Byron and Hobhouse were invited to the palace of Ioannina, where a small grandson, Mahmout Pasha, consented in the absence of his father, Mouctar Pasha, to do the honours. Byron was enchanted by the child's enormous black eyes, 'which our ladies would purchase at any price', and by his naively dignified manner. He asked Byron how he came to be travelling around so young, with no

Lala (tutor) to look after him. 'The question was put by the little man', observed the delighted traveller, 'with all the gravity of three score'.

Byron had already acquired many valuable new experiences in Ioannina, not to mention new clothes: a Suliot 'capote' or thick cloak woven of black, brown or grey local wool, and two magnificent Albanian outfits at fifty guineas each. (You can buy exquisite women's kaftans in Epirus and the Ionian Islands today for less than a fifth of Byron's price.) But they could not find anyone to mend an umbrella, and only one man, an Italian, to make them a new bedstead.

Byron was present in the city during the evening festival following one of the Mohammedan days of Ramadan. This provided him with material both for *Childe Harold* and *The Giaour*. Here are lines from the latter:

> *The crescent glimmers on the hill,*
> *The Mosque's high lamps are quivering still . . .*
> *The flashes of each joyous peal*
> *Are seen to prove the Moslem's zeal.*
> *To-night, sets Rahmazani's sun;*
> *To-night, the Bairam feast's begun . . .*

After nearly a week of shopping and sightseeing, Byron and Hobhouse decided to visit the little man's grandfather, the Lion of Ioannina himself, at distant Tepelene.

4 'Monastic Zitza'

The experiences Byron was to meet with in Tepelene, and on the way there, far outshone anything which Ioannina or little Mahmout could offer. His journey led him through the wildest of mountain passes, then almost untrodden by Europeans. Curiously enough, the passes from Greece into Albania are now once more, 150 years later, equally unknown to visitors. For, as the guidebooks admonish the tourist, it is absolutely impossible to enter Albanian Tepelene from across the Greek frontier.

The first stop for Byron and Hobhouse was Zitza. It was normally a four-hour ride from Ioannina to this hamlet clinging to a mountain-side in the tremendous Pindus range, which forms the spine of north-western Greece. Hobhouse arrived safely by the evening. But Byron for some reason lingered behind. In springtime the mountains are relatively barren; in mid-autumn the rains made them utterly bleak.

Countless small rocks mottled grey and black are scattered among the scrub between low grey stone walls, but in spring the turf between is whitened with sheets of asphodel and gilded with smaller clumps of the yellow snake's-head lily, while there are emerald patches in the scrub where the streams come down. Signs of overgrown furrows remain, as in parts of Ireland, to show that the ground was once tilled. The shepherds build shelters of brown twigs and branches around green bushes for themselves and their sheep in case of emergency.

The emergency struck Byron in the shape of a violent storm. Among the vertical crags a merely drizzly day will produce fantastic wreaths of mist and cloud which suggest the visions of a nightmare. A thunderstorm is supremely daunting. Byron's Greek dragoman and English valet were petrified, the former firing off pistols to summon aid or possibly to frighten away the thunder. Fletcher feared at best starvation and at worst bandits. An anxious Hobhouse, who had not seen Byron for nine hours (though Zitza was only a few miles from where the poet's party were wandering lost), ordered signal-fires to be lit and shots fired. If the wanderers noticed them at all, they can only have seemed like additional bursts of thunder and lightning. Even in the shelter of Hobhouse's 'hovel' the women wept with terror and the men crossed themselves at every peal.

Meanwhile Byron was characteristically amused by his plight. He found a graveyard – always an attraction to him, and Turkish graveyards have a peculiar charm, with their small carved turbans on top of men's tombstones – and there, to the play of lightning, he apostrophised Mrs Spencer Smith as 'Florence':

> *Clouds burst, skies flash, oh, dreadful hour!*
> *More fiercely pours the storm!*
> *Yet here one thought has still the power*
> *To keep my bosom warm.*

In fact it was Byron's Suliot capote, rather than the thought of Mrs Spencer Smith that kept his bosom warm – and dry. You can see the Pindus shep-herds shrugging on their capotes today, whenever rain threatens, while across the grey mountains their closely-packed flocks form strung-out white triangles and lozenges, always speckled with a number of black sheep. A cheerful Byron and his infinitely bedraggled attendants did not reach Zitza until 3 a.m., but the place was worth the struggle to get there.

'Monastic Zitza!' he was to rhapsodise in *Childe Harold*; for it was in the monastery of the Prophet Elias surrounded by oak trees that Byron found a truly warm welcome next day.

> *Monastic Zitza! from thy shady brow,*
> *Thou small, but favoured plot of holy ground!*
> *Where'er we gaze, around, above, below,*
> *What rainbow tints, what magic charms are found ...*

Around, the rocks and forests; above, the bluest of skies after the storm; below, the grey village among its vines, and far below that, a waterfall with a

The town of Ioannina seen across Lake Pambotis.

34

LEFT A gorge near Zitza.

RIGHT A shepherd in the Pindus mountains wearing his capote.

drop of sixty feet in the River Kalamas, which Byron understood to be 'black Acheron', river of the underworld. (In fact, the River Kalamas was the ancient Thyamis, while the Acheron flows through the savage Suli country to the south-east; Byron was later to enter it in dramatic circumstances.) The vertiginous heights and roaring cataract gave to lovely Zitza that peculiar combination of opposites which 'shock yet please the soul'. To be at once shocked and pleased was Byron's idea of heaven.

The Convent of St Elias in which the party now rested, and to which they returned on the way back from Tepelene, has never lost its power to please.

A view through the windows of the monastery of St Elias in Zitza, where Byron's party rested on the way to and from Tepelene.

(Incidentally, in Byron's day monastic buildings which housed monks were often known as 'convents' – a trap for the modern visitor who, on hearing that Byron stayed in a 'convent', cannot be blamed for assuming this to be yet another of Don Juan's escapades.) Over a century and a half after Byron's visit, the monks of St Elias are even more conscious of his presence than were their predecessors of 1809. They point to the now grass-grown corner of the monastery where Byron's guest-room once stood. Perhaps their predecessors gave him 'Turkish Delight' washed down with *ouzo* (as today), in addition to 'pleasant white wine', pressed by hand not foot, which the 'humble meek-mannered' Abbot offered in 1809. (Hobhouse.) They were told that wine made from mountain grapes tasted better than vintages from the plain. Byron certainly climbed the same three semi-circular steps, passed through the same rounded entrance arch, and under the same small belfry; but there was as yet no plaque adorning the bare outer wall. It was placed there in 1924 to mark the hundredth anniversary of the death of 'Lordos Byronos'.

Another fifty years were to pass, and the bell which Byron had heard calling the monks to Mass, was to summon a band of Greek villagers, and of his own compatriots, to a moving service in his memory.

The tiny chapel was brilliant with sixteenth-century frescoes of saints and apostles, the eyes of the military saints, alas, long since put out by Turkish soldiers. A golden mist of candle-light shone on the stars in the dome, as Byron's name was intoned in a litany of praise by the handsome bearded Abbot, amid many *Kyries*, *Alleluias* and *Hosannas*. The duty of the Church, said the Abbot, was to send up a stream of love like the flames of the candles; and Byron's love had conferred a timeless blessing upon Greece.

The villagers of Zitza were no less eager than the monks to remember Byron and to welcome his countrymen. His death had occurred on Easter Monday in April 1824, so that hard-boiled eggs painted a bright crimson were the appropriate refreshments to provide in April 1974. There was also white goat-cheese (which Byron had loved), mountain lamb, fresh bread and the famous Zitza wine, cloudy pink and effervescent.

Byron's visit was too late in the season for Easter eggs. There were a great many more girls, however, wearing their traditional costumes than do so today; the triangular head-shawl with a corner falling over the forehead, or an embroidered cap, or headdress hanging down the back; the long black sleeveless tunic with embroidered edges over a blouse; a coloured apron, full skirt, belt with decorative stitching or plain with a silver buckle, and tinkling cascades of silver ear-rings, bracelets and necklaces.

But in Byron's day Zitza was too poor to manage more than one grape harvest. Its 110 families had to pay crushing Turkish dues and support Ali Pasha's substantial seraglio at one end of the village, plus a Christian bishop and fifteen churches. So poor were the people, indeed, that Byron promised to beg Ali Pasha to cut their taxes. Whether Ali did so, however, he never heard. Some of the grapes, therefore, were unripe when gathered and the wine was sour, watered down and heavily fortified with resin to give it body. Not so today.

5 Ali Pasha, Lion of Ioannina

It took the riders a week to reach Tepelene from Zitza. Scenery every bit as formidable and glorious as the renowned Ravine of Vicos (only a little off the travellers' route) opened before them and closed behind their swaying backs, to disclose yet another vista of unscalable crags on which some monastery had nevertheless been miraculously balanced. The now abandoned

monastery of Vicos makes an admirable setting in which to remember Byron. The long-silent bell is wakened into eerie life; voices shout 'Byron!' across the gorge and Echo makes answer; after rain the river dashing below is a strange pale green, just as Byron and Hobhouse saw the rivers of Epirus, instead of sparkling with the crystal clarity of summer. The scrub oaks in the gorges are lavishly festooned with lichen.

The hazards of negotiating village streets in the Pindus are illustrated by Monodendri. Here the slippery, sloping cobbles are laid in horizontal lines, with a raised line at short intervals, while two vertical rows of cobbles form the edges of the street. Not an easy walk for modern shoes. Nor can it have been easy for Byron's laden horses. Hobhouse, moreover, found the rough sleeping-quarters almost unbearable. Hard boards, damp blankets, wakeful dogs, sleepless bugs, an unappetising dinner with the fowl always 'done to rags' beforehand – these things, and Byron's unshakable insouciance all helped to ruin Hobhouse's nights. He would accuse his friend of 'brutal' indifference – an adjective which later caused Byron to remember that some times they would actually sleep in a cow-byre, when the ejected 'brutes' would

The wild scenery between Zitza and Tepelene: ABOVE mountains snowcapped in April; RIGHT a deserted monastery at the edge of a gorge.

The island in the centre of Lake Pambotis to which Ali Pasha fled in 1822, pursued by Turkish soldiers who shot him to death in the monastery of St Pantaleimon.

butt indignantly on their door. (There are few cows to be seen in the Pindus range today, so perhaps the butting was done by equally indignant goats.)

Notwithstanding his uncomplaining endurance, even Byron was glad to finish at length his 'up-gazing' on towering peaks. The travellers descended towards a cluster of 'glittering minarets', crossed a great river, the ancient Aöus, (known as the Voïoussa in Byron's time) which seemed to them as broad as the Thames at Westminster, though full of gravel banks, and finally faced Tepelene's encircling walls. With infectious gusto Byron was later to describe the hum of Ali Pasha's cosmopolitan army assembled in and around his palace-fort – the high-capped Tartars, wild Albanians, bearded Turks, Moors, red-scarved Macedonians, Turkish Delhi cavalry in terrifying head-dresses, and last but not least, 'the lively, supple Greek'.

Ali Pasha received his guests in a marble-paved pavilion with a fountain playing in the centre to cool the air. The lascivious despot, outwardly so venerable and gentle, attempted with almonds, sherbet and sweet words to seduce the youthful Byron, who in turn had necessarily endeavoured to make a good impression. Out had come his and Hobhouse's formal scarlet uniforms; over to Ali was handed the splendid gift of an elegantly engraved Manton sporting-gun. Ali offered congratulations on the recent surrender of Cephalonia, Ithaca and Zante to Byron's compatriots, and then complimented the handsome youth on his 'small ears, curling hair, & little white hands' – apparently all signs of noble blood. (Ali would not have hesitated to cut off those little ears and hands, if provoked, as he had cut off so many others.)

These compliments naturally did not impress Hobhouse as much as they pleased Byron, and Hobhouse noted sarcastically in his journal how Byron gave him 'a lecture about not caring enough for the English nobility'. (Hobhouse was to become Lord Broughton, so he may in due course have grown to 'care'.)

Byron was aware of Ali's erotic designs. A contemporary print shows the young Englishman sitting uneasily at the end of a cushioned divan, as far away as possible from his host and as close as possible to a group of voluptuous houris. He did not accept Ali's invitation to 'visit him often, and at night when he was more at leisure'. Nor was he unconscious of the blood-thirsty reality concealed beneath the benign exterior. This seemingly mild patriarch, with long white beard and blue eyes, had 'a tiger's tooth'. The poet shrewdly prophesied in *Childe Harold*, Canto II (1812), a bloody fate for the tyrant:

> *Blood follows blood, and through their mortal span,*
> *In bloodier acts conclude those who with blood began.*

A visit by public motor-launch to the fascinating island in Lake Pambotis, opposite Ioannina, will underline the tale of Ali's cruelties and disclose

43

the violent end which did indeed overtake him some ten years after Byron wrote.

The deep fringe of papyrus reeds around the island's shores induces a sense of peace and remoteness. Bull frogs and water fowl begin their evening chorus; lake carp move indolently in the local taverna's glass tank – until they are caught for the tourists' supper. To this island Ali Pasha fled in 1822, after Ioannina had been besieged on the orders of the Sultan. The French Bonaparte had died the year before, and the Sultan had decided it was time for the 'Mahometan Bonaparte', as Ali was called, to meet his death.

Ali took refuge in the island's monastery of St Pantaleimon, whose thick surrounding coverts and spreading plane trees are probably still much as the fugitive saw them. So gigantic is the trunk of one plane tree that you would almost expect to find the signatures of Byron and Hobhouse among the many names carved in its bark. Simple in the extreme, this monastery has yellow-washed walls, outside stone staircases and a wooden balcony with rails. Inside is a museum exhibiting costumes of the period, weapons, braziers, hubble-bubbles, rugs, cushions and dramatic prints. A portrait of 'Lordos Byrònos' presides over a pictorial display of Ali Pasha's pleasures and more notable crimes.

Here is the harem, all bustle and apparent contentment; here is Kyra Frossyni with sleek dark hair and glamorous painted eyes; here is Ali Pasha at his most innocent, being rowed by his slaves on this very lake, a thoroughly fraudulent representation of a tyrant looking like Santa Claus; and here is the dark night, the sinister boat, the Lady Frossyni rolling her tragic black eyes as she is about to be sewn up in a sack and thrown to the eels and water-snakes of Lake Pambotis. Byron was to see for himself something of that Turkish custom of drowning women in sacks. It shocked him profoundly – even though he was twice voluntarily to attend public executions in London.

Ali's end was cleaner than Kyra Frossyni's. The soldiers of the Sultan chased him to the island and shot him up, literally, through the monastery floor. Four large round bullet-holes can be seen to this day in the floor-boards. To a sceptical observer, however, they are suspiciously like the holes which might be left by removing knots in the wood.

Winding, cobbled alleys lead down from the scene of Ali Pasha's assassination to a group of medieval Greek churches nearer the landing-stage. Again the walls and domes, as at Zitza, are emblazoned with frescoes of gold, red and blue. A horrifying martyrdom of St Nicholas – teeth being pulled out with ghastly realism while daggers enter every inch of his body – is matched in ferocity of feeling only by the evidences of Turkish barbarism. Many faces have been shot away and are mere blurs of plaster. Most touching is the tiny cellar known as the 'Underground School' in a cramped, windowless space beneath one of the churches, like a World War II domestic air-raid shelter, where the Greek children of Ioannina were secretly taught by their priests to spell out their own forbidden native tongue. Under the rule of Ali Pasha himself, however, the Greek language was encouraged, since he needed Greek support against his Turkish overlords.

During the third week of October 1809, Byron and Hobhouse returned from Tepelene to Ioannina, where there were various amusements, including a Turkish puppet-show which Hobhouse found 'too horribly gross to be described'. Another black-eyed grandson of Ali's helped to entertain them at the palace. Mahmout, and now this twelve-year-old Hussein Bey, seemed to Byron 'the prettiest little animals I ever saw'.

In some senses Byron himself was a 'pretty animal'. He had the winning ways of a child of nature, as well as the child's spontaneous gaiety alternating with moods of withdrawal. But now he was to be a poet, with all the self-discipline that such a change entailed. His verses would no longer be the product of mere 'Hours of Idleness'. His biographer tells us that his travels in Greece had awakened in him a burning need 'to sift the impressions of his youth'. His life might seem 'purposeless': the writing of poetry would give it direction. And so, on 31 October 1809, three days before leaving Ioannina for the south, Byron began to compose *Childe Harold's Pilgrimage*.

He had at first thought of calling his hero *'Childe Burun'* – Burun being supposedly an antique or Norman form of Byron. But 'Harold' he became, perhaps because English Harold's pedigree went back even beyond the Norman Conquest, and he had a melancholy end:

> *And now Childe Harold was sore sick at heart …*
> *Apart he stalked in joyless reverie,*
> *And from his native land resolved to go,*
> *And visit scorching climes beyond the sea;*
> *With pleasure drugged, he almost longed for woe,*
> *And e'en for change of scene would seek the shades below.*

6 'Robbers All at Parga'

Byron's next 'change of scene' was to be indeed a woeful one: he only just avoided 'the shades below', or, in Fletcher's words, a watery grave.

Having reached Prevesa again on the way southwards, he and Hobhouse decided to accept an offer made by Ali Pasha of a Turkish ship to carry them to Patras. The rains had ceased and the autumn sun was as hot as midsummer in England. The sea voyage would cut out the robber-infested mountains. Unfortunately, out of a crew of forty, only four of them – all Greeks – knew how to handle a fifty-ton vessel in a high wind. Abandoning all hope of reaching Patras, the fatalistic Turkish captain allowed his ship to drive north

The castle and rocky coast of Parga.

towards Corfu. Even this goal proved beyond him, and during the night he handed over his command to the Greeks. Meanwhile the foresail had split, the main-yard had snapped, the guns had broken loose and the ship, rolling heavily, echoed with wild cries for succour to Allah, the saints, and on Fletcher's part to his far-distant wife.

After trying in vain to hearten his valet, Byron 'lay down on deck to wait the worst'. He had learned to 'philosophise' on his travels, as he told his mother in a spirited account of the crisis. What perhaps helped him most to 'philosophise' was again his warm Suliot capote, which he wrapped around himself. This was the second time his Suliot capote had come in handy. The words 'Souliote' and 'capote' were also to provide him with a handy pair of rhymes:

> *Oh! who is more brave than a dark Souliote,*
> *In his snowy camese and his shaggy capote?*

46

On other occasions the invaluable garment could be rhymed with 'note' 'boat' 'goat' and 'remote'. For the capote finds its way into many Byronic situations: Conrad the Corsair sees that his capote is 'lightly slung' on his shoulders before dashing off to attack Seyd Pasha; and the fate of Selim in *The Bride of Abydos* is revealed by something stained red and tangled with the seaweed on the beach, beside a broken torch and oarless boat – 'There lies a white capote!'

Byron's crisis was solved by the four skilful Greek sailors, who anchored safely at 1 a.m. in the bay of Fanari on the rocky Suliot coast. They were rescued by a Suliot chieftain who took them to a 'miserable cottage' for the rest of the night. At dawn they could see the southern tip of Corfu and the Islands of Paxos and Antipaxos out to sea, behind them the castle of Suli, and on the distant shore the town of Parga. A wide bay of smooth wet sand curved away below them. Today the bay is backed by a forest of unusually large olive trees, so heavily laden that nets are spread to catch the fruit. Steep narrow lanes thread their way between the olives and orange groves. At the south end of the bay is a pine-covered promontory crowned by an imposing Norman castle, whose battlements and turrets vie in ferocity with the many fangs of rock which jut out of the sea, to gnash this perilous but enchanting coast. It bears an exhilarating likeness to the Cornish coves of Byron's Trevanion ancestors.

Parga in those days was familiar only to the wild fraternity of Suliot warriors. 'Robbers all at Parga' was a chorus which Byron and Hobhouse were soon to hear chanted around camp fires in the hills, where goats were roasted on spits. Fletcher thought less than nothing of its beauties. 'Bless you! there is very little country', he confided to Trelawny many years later; 'it's all rocks and robbers. They live in holes in rocks, and come out like foxes; they have long guns, pistols and knives. . . . They drink a stuff they call wine, but it tastes more of turps than grapes, and is carried about in stinking goat-skins. . . .'

Today Parga bids fair to be a queen of resorts. There are no more robbers, not even in the cafés and shops along the front, where bills are presented with rectitude and all information about roads through the vast mountainous hinterland is accurate and helpful. If they tell you that a mountain-road is safe for cars, it is. But Parga's beauty is still as vivid and picturesque as when Byron's party threw themselves on the mercy of its Albanian tribesmen in November 1809.

The Suliot chieftain who succoured the travellers at Fanari turned out to be exactly the kind of 'noble savage' whom Byron admired most. He refused all payment – 'No, I wish you to love me, not to pay me.' Byron's love for this romantic and gallant race did indeed grow swiftly. The Suliots had success-fully defied the all-conquering Ali Pasha up till six years before, when their stronghold in the Acarnanian crags behind Parga was treacherously sold to

the Turks. Many Suliots were massacred, a few got away, but the majority took refuge in the monastery of Zalongo. Ali's soldiers, who did not recognise the right of Christian asylum, again attacked and killed the remainder, all except sixty Suliot women. These women escaped with their babies in their arms. They gathered near a precipice. Suddenly someone began to chant one of the heroic Suliot songs. The line advanced towards the edge of the chasm in a trance of patriotic exaltation. One by one the women hurled themselves and their children to freedom and death.

The Suliot survivors were in Byron's time living as refugees in the Ionian Islands, or as prisoners on the island of Ioannina in Lake Pambotis, or had

Suli country near Paramithia.

The wilds of Acarnania where Byron and Hobhouse spent their nights round the campfires of singing and dancing banditti.

taken to their native hills and harbours such as Parga, where Byron found some of them.

No wonder Byron's spirits continued to lift in this wilderness of marvellously beautiful rock and scrub. His road passed beneath the cliffs where stood the ruins of Zalongo, today marked by a challenging modern monument to the Suliot women. An ever-varying panorama of limestone crags unfolds above the traveller's head, while the watered valleys are grey with olives, green with wild figs and rosy pink with Judas trees in the spring. When Byron and Hobhouse passed through it was October and the gorges of the Acheron, located here and not at Zitza, would have begun to make their

49

sinister river look black. But on the fertile coastal plain south-west of Parga the late maize crop was still being harvested, while many kinds of fragrant shrubs were covered with berries, and the lovely strawberry tree dangled its scarlet clusters over their path.

In the heart of this superb Suli country lies Paramithia, high on the slopes of Mt Korillas. Its Venetian fort is ruined, but its name means 'consolation'. It can have been little consolation to Byron's Suliots to know that their rugged citadel was now occupied by a flourishing Turkish colony, served by Greek shop-keepers and filled with terraced houses, beautiful gardens, fountains and mosques. In the old days, Hobhouse learnt, the Paramithiots had been notorious for their savagery. A 'Frank' or foreigner from the West, happening to find himself in the market-place, was liable to be sold as a slave.

If a storm blows up in these passes, great swathes of slate-coloured cloud or transparent shreds of mist add beauty to the fantastic mountains. Or there may be total black-out for the moment, with the sound of small bells close by but no sign of goats. Then comes a rent in the storm-cloud; a torrent far below appears as a pale streak of light; and on the turf by the roadside, goats and kids suddenly materialise in a vivid patchwork of brown, black, fawn, tawny and white.

Having returned safely by land to Prevesa, the travellers decided to sail eastwards along the Ambracian Gulf and then make the rest of their way to Patras by land, entrusting themselves to a fifty-strong guard of Albanian freelances, rather than to a crew of law-abiding but unnautical Turks. The size of their bodyguard was by no means excessive. Travelling through this same dangerous country in the same year, Captain Leake took a bodyguard of forty Albanian soldiers.

Their second vision of Actium Bay by moonlight produced from Byron a poem to his current Cleopatra, namely Mrs 'Florence' Spencer Smith. But his note was, as ever, light not tragic. Dismissing the attractive thought that 'Florence's' charms might create many new Anthonys – the world was no longer the same as it had been in 31 BC – he wrote:

> Though Fate forbids such things to be,
> Yet, by thine eyes and ringlets curled!
> I cannot lose a world for thee,
> But would not lose thee for a world.

It was in the western wilds of 'Acarnania's forests wide' and 'Aetolia's wolds', between Prevesa and Missolonghi, that Byron and Hobhouse spent their famous nights out with their friendly banditti, whose twin 'solaces', according to Leake, were to take snuff and play cards around the camp fires. Byron, however, was privileged to watch the men dancing: 'bounding hand in hand, man linked to man' – a national and historic dance which he almost certainly saw again fourteen years later, in the Ionian island of Cephalonia.

Part of the lagoon which stretches from Anatolica to Missolonghi. The causeway is modern.

A description of the bounding and singing, the shouts and screams, found its way into *Childe Harold*, with a final rousing call to 'Tambourgi', the Suliot drummer:

> *Tambourgi! Tambourgi! thy larum afar*
> *Gives hope to the valiant, and promise of war;*
> *All the sons of the mountains arise at the note,*
> *Chimariot, Illyrian, and dark Souliote! . . .*
>
> *Then the pirates of Parga that dwell by the waves,*
> *And teach the pale Franks what it is to be slaves,*
> *Shall leave on the beach the long galley and oar,*
> *And track to his covert the captive on shore.*

Robbery with murder had been committed by a roving band in one of the Acarnanian villages (Utraikee) just before the English party passed through it. But Byron's Albanians acted as faithful gamekeepers against poachers from outside.

They reached Missolonghi on 20 November, having been prepared for the strange beauties of its salt lagoon by their previous night's stop at the village of Anatolico, which was situated north of Missolonghi on the same vast lagoon. Both Anatolico and Missolonghi were relatively poor at the time, since the Napoleonic wars increasingly interfered with commerce and threw their sailors out of work. Missolonghi, unlike Actium Bay or the lovely Ambracian Gulf, inspired Byron with no effervescence on the subject of 'Sweet Florence', or indeed of anything else.

7 'Delphi's Sacred Side'

They were back in Patras again on 22 November. This time they had more leisure to note the rich orchards and vineyards, the licorice plants growing up the hillsides – and the pleasing 'novelties' of tables and chairs. Their Greek friends told them that the old Turkish fortress was perfectly useless, being put into a 'state of defence' at the beginning of every war by a coat of white-wash.

Byron and Hobhouse could now plan their longed-for next move: the visit to Athens, of which Byron had already notified his mother. He would spend the winter in Athens, studying modern Greek. 'I have no desire to return to England. . . .' On 4 December they started off eastwards along the rough, stony southern shore of the Gulf of Corinth, and then through groves of ripe oranges and lemons as far as Vostitza, the modern Aigion, jutting out on a tongue of fertile land into the Gulf. Here they found a cornucopia of fruits and vegetables: quinces, medlars, pomegranates, melons, cauliflowers, spinach, artichokes and celery. Here Byron had three memorable experiences.

At Vostitza he shot his last wild bird, an eaglet, whose dying eyes made him resolve never to shoot another. This was the tender-hearted Byron who had previously mourned over 'the wild plunging of the tortured horse' at a Spanish bull-fight. At Vostitza he also had his first glimpse of Greek nationalism. Young Andreas Londos, the delightfully animated twenty-year-old Greek governor of Vostitza under the Turks, with a face like a chimpanzee, was so much stirred when the name of Rhiga, an earlier Greek political martyr, cropped up in casual conversation, that he leapt from a sofa, knocked over a draught-board, burst into tears and broke into Rhiga's national anthem, *Greeks Arise!* It was the enthusiasm of Londos which kindled Byron's interest in the struggle for Greek freedom. And at Vostitza Byron got his first sight of Mount Parnassus across the Corinthian Gulf.

A view of the Parnassus range across the Corinthian Gulf between Patras and Aigion. This would have been Byron's first sight of Mount Parnassus.

The Delphi valley, looking towards the town of Itea in the distance.
Either side of the River Pleistos lie carpets of olive trees.

Oh thou, Parnassus! whom I now survey,
Not in the frenzy of a dreamer's eye,
Not in the fabled landscape of a lay,
But soaring snow-clad through thy native sky,
In the wild pomp of mountain majesty!

This was the noble route, the route by Parnassus, which the travellers were to take to Athens, not the shorter one by the Isthmus of Corinth. The longer road would lead them through Delphi.

The summit of Mount Parnassus can be scaled only during July and August. Most travellers will therefore see it just as Byron saw it, snow-clad. Its whole magnificent range dominates this part of Greece, as Pindus dominates the north-west. Indeed, from its crown can be seen the great mountains of Greece whose names are myth, legend and history in one: to the north-west Pindus itself; Callidromus, Oeta, Pelion, Ossa and Olympus to the north; Helicon and Cithaeron to the south-east; and the mountains of the Peloponnese to the south.

Byron crossed once more to the northern shore, somewhat west of the modern ferry-service. Today passengers land direct at Itea, at the head of the Krisaean Gulf. Byron and Hobhouse were rowed over in a strong Cephaloniot ten-oared boat, winding in and out of the many rocky bays which line the Krisaean Gulf, skirting Galaxidhi, where they saw the masts of anchored merchant vessels swaying in the moonlight, and finally reaching at midnight the 'scale' or port for Salona, now Itea. Here they slept malodourously in an onion shed. Byron was to make many efforts to reach the inland town of Salona itself from Missolonghi, in 1824; but fate was against him.

From Itea begins a drive of extraordinary beauty: the steep direct route to Delphi. At the bottom of the valley runs the River Pleistos; on either side unrolls a most magnificent carpet of immense olives. These groves have been likened to a 'sea of olives' flowing between Delphi and the Gulf. But to anyone who has visited Arachova, the next village beyond Delphi on the road towards Athens, the olives in the Pleistos valley resemble nothing so much as one of the splendid tufted rugs which are Arachova's pride.

Byron and his party made for Chrisso, on the way to Delphi. 'The last part of our ride was up an ascent', wrote Hobhouse, 'for Crisso is placed on the roots of Parnassus.' The path was so steep they had to keep dismounting from their horses. Here and there were the entrances to caves, in which were stone troughs for coffins. Above them were the precipitous limestone rocks veined with white marble, the home of eagles, vultures, kites and in Byron's day wolves; it was here that he saw his flight of twelve 'eagles'. He took them as a sign that Apollo and the muses who lived on Parnassus had accepted his offering of *Childe Harold*. This cheered him, even though Hobhouse had to announce (probably correctly) that they were not eagles but only Egyptian vultures. As it was winter Byron saw the River Pleistos as full and foaming

as it ever became; in early summer it looks a mere trickle among sandbanks. But the sides of the ravine make up for the lack of water by a golden surcoat of flowers – broom, mullein, spurge, daisies with orange rays and Jerusalem sage. A pair of buzzards wheel in wide circles from side to side of the glen, slowly weaving their way up the valley towards their nest in the crags.

Sad to relate, the antiquities of Delphi were a disappointment to Byron. Perhaps they had been over-exposed in advance, so to speak, by Hobhouse's enthusiasm. Byron, too, was soaked in the classics. At seven he had demanded books from his mother on Greece and Turkey – and little was known during his childhood about contemporary Greece. The headmaster of Harrow found him a rewarding classical pupil. But when Byron saw far-famed

Ruins of the temple of Minerva and the Castalian Spring were among the sights of Delphi visible in Byron's day, but they failed to impress him.

Fir forests cover
the lower ranges of the
Parnassus mountains.

Delphi and realised that it was now no more than an overgrown amphitheatre, another cave on the way to the Stadium, a few pillars of the Gym-
nasium and Temple of Minerva below the Sacred Way, and marble rubble
scattered in the mud around the hovels of Castri village, his spirits drooped.
Even the Castalian Spring could not revive him, though it bubbled out at
the foot of a huge cleft in the rocks as lively as ever, filling its stone troughs
beneath niches for votive offerings and sprinkling the travellers with its spray.
Byron pronounced it to have 'a villanous [sic] twang'. (Dr Chandler, an
earlier traveller, was said to have contracted a fever simply from washing his
hands in it.)

After he and Hobhouse had carved their names on a pillar of the Gym-
nasium (still visible) he felt he had paid all necessary respects to Delphi.

Incidentally they also discovered two signatures, 'H. P. Hope, 1799' and
'Aberdeen, 1803'. It was even more agreeable, decided Hobhouse, to come
upon the names of two fellow countrymen like these, than a couple of ancient
Greek inscriptions.

The entrance to the Castalian Spring in Byron's day was singularly bare,
adorned only by some wild shrubs and a tangle of ivy and saxifrage. Today
there are still the wild rock plants but also belts of poplar and pine, hedges of
lilac and Judas, quince and crab apple, and trellises of wistaria.

Could the disconsolate Byron have known of the wonders which lay
buried beneath his feet, to be excavated by the French towards the end of the
century, his reactions to Delphi's ruins might have been different. To his
credit, Captain Leake suspected the existence of hidden masterpieces. What
would Byron have said to the bronze Charioteer, a youthful aristocrat like
himself, with eyes of onyx and a look of sublime detachment, as he crowns
his victory by driving his winning team slowly around the Stadium for all to
admire and applaud? Or to the Argive twins, Cleobis and Biton, whose
poor widowed mother was drawn by them in a chariot all the way from Argos
to Delphi? She asked Hera, queen of the gods, to reward her devoted sons.
Hera acquiesced, for the boys lay down in the temple of Delphi to sleep and
never woke up. Those whom the gods love die young – as it might be,
Shelley and Byron.

The statuette of a small girl has a charmingly complacent smile, reminiscent of Byron's wife Annabella. And beyond the museum in which these
and many other precious 'finds' are displayed, lie the various Treasuries of the
Greek City States, winding up the Sacred Way towards the great Temple
of Apollo. Here the 'Pythoness', or Delphic priestess, chewed her laurel
leaves, sniffed mephitic vapours from a rock, drank special water, or whatever else she did to promote her 'trips', and gave oracular advice. She had
to be a woman over fifty years of age in order to ensure her chastity. One
thinks of Byron's future friend Lady Melbourne. If not chaste at fifty, she
befriended him chastely at sixty-two, and gave him much advice, both good

RIGHT The Pindus range
of mountains.

OVERLEAF, LEFT Crags abov[e]
the Sacred Way at Delphi.
RIGHT Remains of
the stadium at Delphi.

and bad. Above the Temple lies the Amphitheatre of Dionysus, of which Byron had seen only a trace; and beyond that, the magnificent Stadium, though in 1809 only the upper rows of seats were still above ground. It is hardly surprising that Byron was disappointed.

There is a tenacious tradition which associates Parnassus with Byron in a more cheerful mood. The Mayor of Delphi in April 1974 remembered being taken as a small boy to see a second Byronic signature, but this time in the stone over the entrance to the celebrated Corycian Cave, described by the ancient historian, Pausanias. The outer chamber of this allegedly forty-roomed cavern is two hundred feet long, glistening with stalagmites and stalactites and filled with a curious light that is sometimes pink, sometimes green. It has been a famous place of refuge since time immemorial – or at any rate, since the last of the nymphs or Maenads romped on these mountains with Pan or Dionysus. The cave was used by Greeks as a hide-away from the Persians in the fifth century, from the Turks in the War of Independence, and from the Germans in World War II. However, Byron's biographer, Professor Marchand, does not believe he spent long enough at Delphi to visit this cave, situated as it is about seven miles distant on the flank of Mount Liakura.

It is true that the travellers arrived in Delphi on 16 December, returned to Chrisso for the night and left on the 17th. They might possibly have accomplished the detour northwards to the cave if they had gone direct from Delphi to Arachova, since it is equidistant between them. Once you have made the climb, writes Leake, 'the access from each place is easy'. Nor was Byron one to omit such a visit if it were suggested to him. He seems to have been as much addicted to caves as he was bored or angered by ruins. Both on Mt Parnes above Athens and on Ithaca, he plunged into a cave, incidentally getting seriously lost in the former. But tempting as it is to imagine Byron bathed in that pinkish-green light, one has to admit that he did not mention the Corycian Cave in poetry or prose.

Hobhouse indeed wrote of it, but only to say that the summits of Parnassus were inaccessible: 'They ... could be ascended on horseback for the most part of the way, as far, as least, as the great Corycian cave, which evaded the search of the famous English traveller [Wheler], and has not, that I know of, been ever discovered.'

Even if Byron did not ride up to the Corycian Cave and see from the rough platform below its entrance the magical vision of Itea and the sea on his right, and the mountains on his left – even so, there were scenes of matchless beauty to hold him around Delphi. Beyond the twin peaks of Parnassus, the Old Man and the Wolf, lay range upon range of incomparable crag and colour. Up there every tinge of deep blue and purple creeps into the chasms and crevices, while the snow-fields are constantly changing colour under the passing clouds: blinding white in sunshine, creamy in the shade. Below the

The Parnassus range seen across the Corinthian Gulf near Aigion.

snow-line are mysterious sheets of violet, peacock and green, with tawny tracks and grey rock striped or patched with pink. Scattered fir forests lie in belts of heavy green across the lower slopes. And waiting for the spring are the miniature bulbs of black, emerald and lemon alpine irises and of sky-blue anemones, with the myriad seeds of milkwort to make a more intense and spreading carpet of blue.

The citizens of modern Delphi are very conscious of Byron, particularly of his association with liberal causes. They dream of Delphi as it once was, 'the navel of the world', where Apollo and Dionysus, the spirit and the body, each holds sway for a due period: Apollo for nine months, Dionysus for three months of the year. They remember also that not so long ago Delphi might have been the spiritual centre of the Council of Europe. The ancient Amphictyonic League which met at intervals in Delphi they see as a precur-sor of the United Nations. The Mayor said: 'Byron was not carried away by a limited archeolatry. With his great love, he embraced the whole of historic Hellenism. His Philhellenism comprises in equivalent proportions the totality of the everlasting Greek Nation.'

When the ghosts of Byron the poet and Hobhouse the politician return to walk on Parnassus, civic Delphi believes that the living generations will be free men and women, no longer dwelling even metaphorically in caves.

8   *Across the Boeotian Plain to Attica*

It was now time to descend from the heights and make for Athens, if the travellers were to see the Acropolis by Christmas. They returned to Chrisso, as described, and began on 17 December to climb again up the narrow valley of the Pleistos, from which they could at last see the very crest of Parnassus – a sight to agitate the minds of the ancients, thought Hobhouse, with 'a mingled commotion of piety and fear.' After four hours they reached wine-making, rug-weaving Arachova, high up on its limestone platforms and terraces carved out of the Parnassus massif. Hobhouse called it 'the most considerable town on Liakura', which it still is, though then there were only 350 houses, all inhabited by Greeks. The Greeks danced for them to the accompaniment of a thunderous drum and squeaking pipe. In return Byron's two Albanian servants whirled around, dropped, and rebounded from their knees with a shout.

Then came the long descent between sharp precipices and stony slopes into the wide Boeotian plain, the huge bulk of Parnassus slowly diminishing until at last it was impossible to distinguish its quilt of shining cumulus cloud from its shoulders of snow. At some point they saw a deposit of the legendary clay out of which Prometheus made man, and also the nine-acre

A valley near Livadia.

grave of the giant Tityus. Byron may have stopped beneath the poplars and aspens of Karakolithos for a glass of white Arachova wine. The village was presented by Lord Elgin, Byron's Scottish compatriot, with a clock-tower, perhaps as conscience money for shipping the Acropolis marbles to England.

Elgin did not complete this project until 1812. In the meantime, while Byron was still in Greece, controversy raged over Elgin's 'vandalism' (alternatively, his cultural rescue operation). Needless to say, Byron thundered against Elgin, calling him the last and worst 'dull spoiler' of Athena's treasures. One cannot but agree with Professor Marchand's judgment: 'Byron felt what Hobhouse and others could not foresee: that the Greeks might some day gain their freedom and preserve their own monuments.' Nor is it ever too late for Britain to adopt the proposal of Sir Harold Nicolson – another great Byronist – and present a Caryatid, if only by way of token restitution, to the Acropolis Museum.

Continuing his journey to Athens, Byron saw the famous Triple Way, that ill-omened place where Oedipus met his father at the intersection of three roads. Murder resulted, followed by incest when Oedipus married his mother. The mythical road-junction is not so obvious today as is the fact that Byron's compatriots are still busy in Greece. An advertisement for 'Aberdeen (Hellas) Ltd' stands on the roadside leading to industrial Livadia. But the impassive shepherdesses still wear their heavy black shawls and skirts, as they tend the many flocks of white and brown sheep.

As he rode into Livadia, Mt Helicon, home of the Nine Muses was on his right. To him, Livadia was mainly remarkable for a meeting with a 'free-thinking' Boeotian bishop who called the Mass *coglioneria* – cant. 'It was impossible to think better of him for this', remarked Byron severely. Hob-house was more irritated by the difficulty of attaching names to places in Boeotia, and indeed throughout Greece. 'What do you call that river?' he would ask, to be told, 'The river.' In passing Byron noted the 'nominal' Cave of Triphonius in the side of Livadia's castle hill; the authoritative traveller Captain Leake shared Byron's scepticism about the connection of this shal-low cave with the famous Oracle of Triphonius, son of the King of Orchomenos – or son of Apollo. Byron also visited Orchomenos and the once battle-scarred plain of Plataea with Mt Cithaeron now on his right, haunt of Pan; and Chaeronea, with its fabulous lion erected in memory of the Boeotians killed by the victorious Philip of Macedon in 338 BC. At Orchomenos he saw a visitors' book in which an anonymous fellow-traveller had written a distasteful verse. Byron wrote underneath:

> The modest bard, like many a bard unknown
> Rhymes on our names, but wisely hides his own;
> But yet, whoe'er he be, to say no worse,
> His name would bring more credit than his verse.

The basilica at Orchomenos.

According to Captain Leake, Lord Elgin's hired excavators tried to operate upon the Treasury of Minyas at Orchomenos, but the masses of stone defeated them. Hobhouse, not generally frivolous, recorded their visit to the shepherd Demetrius, 'fat man' of Orchomenos, who spent all day up to his neck in a river during the summer to keep cool.

At last the travellers rode up the hill into Thebes. They had seen it from a distance surrounded by cypresses and mosques. An elegant little museum now enhances the appearance of its dumpy Frankish tower, where marble carvings and mosaics lean against its brown sides. The museum boasts a harvest of golden necklaces and bracelets, with seals of lapis lazuli, brought by Theban merchants from Anatolia. Hobhouse says they lodged two nights

in Thebes at the house of a Greek bishop who showed them the Fountain of
Dirce and the ruins of the poet Pindar's house. Was this the same unorthodox,
perhaps pagan bishop whom Byron remembered meeting in Livadia?

The name of Thebes brought to Byron's mind the brilliant general and
incorruptible hero, Epaminondas, just as the name Thermopylae always
recalled to him King Leonidas of Sparta who, with his three-hundred
Lacedaemonians, died defending the pass into Greece against the hosts of
Xerxes the Persian. When would Greece again produce heroes such as these
to defy the Turk?

> *Ah! Greece! they love thee least who owe thee most;*
> *Their birth, their blood, and that sublime record*
> *Of hero sires, who shame thy now degenerate horde!*

The Greeks of 1809 seemed to Byron 'degenerate' because they accepted the Turkish yoke. Little did he know how soon they were to throw it off.

Thermopylae he might have passed through if he had taken the eastern route back from Ioannina to Athens. The heroic tragedy of Thermopylae, caused by a Greek traitor, inspired him to write of,

> *The hopeless warriors of a willing doom,*
> *In bleak Thermopylae's sepulchral strait –*

Today the blue seas of the strait, with the lovely island of Euboea seen from the coast road, are far from 'sepulchral'. Nor is Thermopylae, famous in ancient times for its hot springs and salt ponds, 'bleak', though the precipitous cliffs of Mt Callidromon and Mt Oeta still crowd in upon it – perhaps not quite 'bleak' enough. A fast modern motor road sweeps past its foothills. On one side of the motorway is a shining white monument to King Leonidas erected by a modern monarch, King Paul of Greece. On the other side of the busy road – if you can reach the other side – is the grass-grown hillock under which the Spartans were buried. Here stands another, quite small memorial of grey stone, more in keeping with Byron's idea of the scene.

Who does not envy Byron's first rapturous vision of Athens? He celebrated it both in prose and verse. It was Christmas Day, 1809. They stood on a small rise near the ruins of the ancient Fort Phyle, then called the Watch Tower, at the gateway to the Attic plain. A guide suddenly called out, '*Affendi, Affendi, to chorio*' – 'Sir, Sir, the town!' Through the fir trees Byron saw a never-to-be-forgotten landscape: 'the Plain of Athens, Pentelicus, Hymettus, the Aegean, and the Acropolis burst upon the eye at once. . . .' Writing after he had visited many other famous panoramas, such as the Trojan plain with Mt Athos, the Hellespont and Constantinople, he still gave the crown to Attica: 'in my opinion, a more glorious prospect than even Cintra and Istambol'.

Later that day he and Hobhouse could distinguish, glittering afar off, the Museion hill crowned by the marble monument to Caius Julius Philopappos, Athenian citizen and Roman consul of the second century AD; the wonderfully preserved Theseum built of Parian marble with a solitary palm standing near it just outside the city walls; Hadrian's Arch; and the sixteen remaining columns of the vast Temple of Olympian Zeus, on one of whose empty bases Byron was to sit and muse:

> *Here let me sit upon this massy stone,*
> *The marble column's yet unshaken base!*

Streets and houses had not yet begun to spill out beyond the ten-foot high city walls into the Attic plain. For Athens was a poor Turkish town. A few people, carts and animals could be seen wandering about the fields, but the eye was not distracted for long by such small domestic matters. It leapt

The Parthenon.

LEFT Cape Sounion with the Temple of
Poseidon on the promontory.

ABOVE Byron inscribed his name on a pillar
of the temple during his visit in 1810.

LEFT The present-day
view from Fort Phyle
across the Attic Plain
to Athens bears no
resemblance to Byron's
first glimpse of the city
from this same spot
in 1809.

straight from Mt Lycabettus, with its ancient chapel of St George, to the
rock-bound heights of the Acropolis. As the travellers rode forward across
the plain, the famous amethyst light that heralds sunset began to flow from
Mt Hymettus. Suddenly the olive groves, the vineyards, the green cornfields,
the cypresses and the waters of 'meek Cephisus' were all dark. Byron noted
how short was the twilight over Greece.

RIGHT The columns of
the Temple of Olympian
Zeus with the Acropolis
in the distance

At close quarters the Athens of Byron was more poignant than romantic.
A 'brisk' walk took Hobhouse right round its walls in a mere forty-seven
minutes. It had a population of only some 10,000; its famous Cephisus
Hobhouse called 'a sort of ditch-stream'. As for the Acropolis, Lord Elgin
had already got to work. Moreover, a massive jumble of fragments had long
covered the plateau, enough to make the present disposition of fallen blocks
look sparse and tidy. It was thus from a petrified sea of broken marble that
arose the glories of Athena's hill; the Propylaea, the Parthenon and the
Erechtheum, their outlines blurred and still more cluttered by white-washed
cottages, huts and sheds, a dungeon, batteries of cannon, and goats which
found shelter beneath the Caryatids.

Yet who would not now gladly settle for that picturesque jumble, on
condition that the muddle contributed by succeeding generations were
removed? From Phyle across the plain the view is no longer of minarets but of
pylons, not of pillars but of factory chimneys. Motorways, motels and filling-
stations reach out from the suburbs to the scented foothills. Only the upper
slopes of the mountain ring have remained, so far, relatively inviolate. Only

The caryatids on the south porch of the Erechtheum. Lord Elgin was so delighted with the figures that he took one to London, together with the frieze of the Parthenon, replacing her with a plaster cast.

the loftiest landmarks in the plain, such as the Acropolis itself, the Areopagus and Museion hills and Mt Lycabettus are able to dominate the tower blocks and other multi-storey competitors. That said, it is still an inspiring experience to gaze at Athens from any of the heights either inside or outside the city. But not from Byron's Phyle.

In *Childe Harold*, Phyle reminded Byron of the servitude which had been clamped down by the Turks upon Athens:

> *Spirit of Freedom! when on Phyle's brow*
> *Thou satst with Thrasybulus and his train,*
> *Couldst thou forbode the dismal hour which now*
> *Dims the green beauties of thine Attic plain?*

Thrasybulus, a classical Greek patriot, had set out from his vantage ground at Phyle to expel the Thirty Tyrants from Athens and re-establish democracy. Who would expel the tyrants from Athens now – not just thirty of them, but the whole crushing 'scourge of Turkish hand'?

> *Who now shall lead thy scattered children forth,*
> *And long accustomed bondage uncreate?*

Byron could not know that he himself was to be part of the answer to that question. Together with the leaders in the War of Independence, he would 'uncreate' Greek bondage.

Meanwhile, however, the fatalistic submission of the Greeks to Turkish bondage was to weigh heavily upon his spirits during his first months in Athens:

> *Ancient of days! august Athena! where,*
> *Where are the men of might? the grand in soul?*
> *Gone – glimmering through the dream of things that were . . .*

Combined with what he called his own 'moping fits', the Greek predicament formed a melancholy, albeit sometimes congenial, undercurrent to all his sightseeing:

> *Greece is no lightsome land of social mirth;*
> *But he whom Sadness sootheth may abide,*
> *And scarce regrets the region of his birth,*
> *When wandering slow by Delphi's sacred side,*
> *Or gazing o'er the plains where Greek and Persian died.*

'Where Greek and Persian died' was of course the plain of Marathon.

9 'The Mountains Look on Marathon'

Marathon, which the travellers visited from Athens on 24 January 1810, epitomised for Byron all that was glorious, sad and nostalgic in human history. It was sad, for instance, to find the village of Marathon inhabited not by Greeks but by a few Turks. Byron responded with many bursts of poetry, culminating in verses of soaring genius and renown.

First, in *Childe Harold* he spoke of 'gray Marathon' being spared, while time and age had laid low Athena's towers and temples. That indeed remains a universal impression. Compared with the noble desolation of the Parthenon, Marathon today seems untouched by time, ever since Darius the Persian was defeated there in 490 BC. It need not always look quite so 'gray', however, as Byron saw it. To be sure, the way to Marathon from Athens is strewn even in summer with little grey-leaved flowers camouflaged against scattered stones and boulders, while the grey bones of the mountains stick out everywhere through the sparse pines, shrubs and olives. But the approaches through the Attic fields can also be incandescent with arum lilies cultivated in shining files, or clumps of spurge and cystus. A gleaming reservoir with gulls, plantations, flowers and cafés breaks the journey from Athens. On the plain of Marathon itself, green cypresses lead up to the sandy mound under which lie the calcined bones of the 192 Athenians killed in the battle. At the foot of the mound Captain Leake's servant was to find many small pieces of black flint, thought to be Persian arrow-heads.

One can climb the mound conveniently by four flights of steps, and if it is springtime there will be a carpet of wild flowers on the top: mignonette, woolly stachys, mauve allium and purple convolvulus. Byron, however, saw Marathon on a late afternoon in mid-winter when the grass, sea and mountains would all have looked grey. Grey buffaloes were grazing in the plain and shadowy eels swimming in a fishery by the shore.

Again, his accusing question:

> *What now remaineth here?*
> *What sacred trophy marks the hallowed ground . . . ?*

But his own reply, 'The rifled urn, the violated mound', has since been rendered less bitter. A wide marble pavement with benches and a long low monument, effective in its plainness and fine lettering, stand at the foot of the mound, together with an ancient *stele* (upright slab) bearing the sculptured portrait of an oriental-looking Greek hoplite (foot soldier); and more than one 'sacred trophy' is exhibited in the nearby museum. Quite enough in fact to satisfy Byron, since Mycenaean, Early and Middle Helladic remains have recently been excavated.

The wide crescent of five mountains still 'look on Marathon', just as he

The Athenian burial
mound at Marathon.

saw them, with no modern buildings to deface their individual shapes or
ridicule their evocative names: Agriliki, (Argaliki in Byron's day), Aphoris-
mos, Prophitis Ilias, Kotroni, Stavrokoraki. (Hobhouse, however, who
always had trouble with his place-names, heard that two of them were
called Mt Icarus and Mt Pan.) It was the thought of these mountains which
inspired Byron to his most memorable and pregnant poetry. After *Childe
Harold* was finished, when he was living in Italy – a country also under a
foreign yoke – he inserted into his mocking masterpiece, *Don Juan*, the
incomparable 'Poet's Song':

> *The isles of Greece, the isles of Greece!*
> *Where burning Sappho loved and sung,*
> *Where grew the arts of war and peace, –*
> *Where Delos rose, and Phoebus sprung!*
> *Eternal summer gilds them yet,*
> *But all, except their sun, is set. . . .*
>
> *The mountains look on Marathon –*
> *And Marathon looks on the sea;*
> *And musing there an hour alone,*
> *I dream'd that Greece might still be free;*
> *For standing on the Persians' grave.*
> *I could not dream myself a slave.*

Six thousand Persian invaders had been slain at Marathon. So wherever Byron strolled or stopped to gaze, he was treading on a Persian's grave.

Sounion, or Cape Colonni, at the tip of Attica, had been the object of Byron's pilgrimage the day before. For a moment the classic beauty of Sounion's Doric temple, half-ruined though it was, seems to have softened and gilded the poet's emotions, inhibiting the indignation which was to find full expression next day at Marathon.

> *Place me on Sunium's marbled steep,*
> *Where nothing, save the waves and I,*
> *May hear our mutual murmurs sweep,*
> *There, swan-like, let me sing and die; . . .*

This is almost to 'die upon the midnight with no pain', like Keats. But suddenly, despite the sea, the 'clustering Cyclades' floating upon it, the wood of pine and cedar, the white columns of Poseidon's temple (thought to be Minerva's in Byron's day), the dancing and the wine, a wave of protest swept over him again and he ended his most stirring poem on a note of passionate anger:

> *A land of slaves shall ne'er be mine –*
> *Dash down yon cup of Samian wine!*

The second time Byron visited Sounion he had an encounter with some Greeks who were far from slavish. A posse of Maniot pirates were lurking in the caves beneath the 'marbled steep', and would have robbed and perhaps killed the travellers but for the presence of their armed guard. Even today the Mani who inhabit the rugged hinterland of the Laconian Gulf at the tip of the Peloponnese do not get a good chit from fellow Greeks. 'The Mani!...a terrible lot: wild, treacherous people, knife-drawers – *machievrovgaltes!*' as Patrick Leigh Fermor, author of *The Mani*, was recently told.

Modern Sounion, it must be confessed, induces Byron's earlier hedonistic mood. It is easy to swim in one of Sounion's coves and see nothing but the

The Temple of Poseidon at Sounion.

beauty which Byron saw, without the anger. The water is clear, and far away at the bottom one can see, instead of plastic containers, shelves of non-sharp porous rock festooned with surprisingly non-slip seaweed. The sand is pleasantly gritty. The wine may not be Samian but there is no impulse to dash it down, except down a grateful throat. The kebabs are delicious and the fish is white mullet from the Aegean. The picnic meal of fried octopus, however, which Byron and Hobhouse ate after visiting Sounion tasted 'tough and insipid'.

Today there may be other 'mutual murmurs' besides those of the waves and oneself; but these are the contented murmurs from German, American or African voices as the procession of visitors winds up the steep hill through creeping mountain shrubs, occasional aloes, tiny crimson poppies and tufts of daisies, and moves on to the paved walk, pays its five drachmae a head at the *guichet* and crosses the turf and slabs of grey rock on to the temple platform. Hobhouse says he and Byron had to scale the ruins of a massive ancient wall to reach it.

Here, deeply incised in the nearest pillar, is the name of names. Byron. Around it are some fainter Greek signatures dated 1816, 1818, 1835 – not to mention some bold modern ego-boosters of the 'H.M. Warren' class. Byron and Hobhouse would have seen many earlier ones. Millions of fingers have stroked the Byron signature, until the marble is as smooth and translucent as if Phidias himself had ordered it to be polished. In a slight haze out to sea, the opalescent shapes of Keos and Hagios Georgios, and the more distant layers of pearly rock behind them look, as the poet said, like the 'Islands of the Blessed'.

10   *Maids of Athens*

Byron's first stay of ten weeks in Athens by no means always rose to the tragic intensity of his experiences at Sounion and Marathon. The travellers found lodgings close to the Acropolis in the home of Mrs Tarsia Macri, widow of a Greek who had been British Vice-Consul. We can see from a contemporary sketch that the widow Macri's house was pleasant: three steps up to the door, large windows with three smaller ones above, an attractive edging round the flat roof. We can see from Byron's verses and letters that the widow Macri's three young daughters were more attractive still: Mariana aged fifteen, Katinka fourteen, and Theresa twelve. Byron preferred Theresa, though he professed to be in love with all three: 'I almost forgot to tell you', he wrote to Henry Drury his first tutor at Harrow, 'that I am dying of love of three Greek Girls at Athens. . . .'

In placing twelve-year-old Theresa above her sisters – or even above her older, more beautiful and accomplished cousin Dudu Roque – Byron was only establishing a pattern which he was to follow several years later when he dedicated the seventh edition of *Childe Harold*, Canto 1, to 'Ianthe', the eleven-year-old Lady Charlotte Harley, daughter of Lady Oxford. Indeed the English Charlotte may have reminded him in some subtle way of the Greek Theresa, despite the many physical differences between a black-eyed and a blue-eyed nymph. It was not that Byron felt any sinister attraction for nymphets. But with his turbulent passions, the happiest alternatives seemed to lie between married women and young girls who were still almost children. The former taught him how to play his emotions like obstreperous fish; the very innocence of the 'maids' of Athens or Eyford kept him in check.

Charlotte Harley was the 'Young Peri of the West' whose eyes, 'wild as the gazelle's', would have been too much for him but for the saving fact that when she was thirteen he was exactly twice her age. Theresa might be called the 'Young Peri of the East' whose 'wild eyes like the roe' brought to him 'love's alternate joy and woe'. (In due course Leila in *The Giaour* was to have eyes 'languishingly dark' like the gazelle.)

A full length, coloured print of the nineteen-year-old Dudu shows how entrancing a beautiful, well-educated Athenian girl could be. Her sloe-eyes and long black hair are set off by a white bodice, gold and white striped skirt, blue and red spotted sash, blue and white shawl. It was Dudu who helped Byron to translate Greek poems; but Theresa has irrevocably captured the mythology.

When Byron was not sparkling in the dewy company of Athenian maids, he was going to parties in Greek or Frankish (Western European) society. One talented Frank was Signor Giovanni Lusieri, the Neopolitan whose exquisite water-colour drawings of Athens and its plain tell us what it all looked like in Byron's day. Lord Elgin may be forgiven much for having employed Lusieri as his artistic agent.

Byron's party-going was balanced by a rigorous schedule of exercise. His favourite ride southwards was to the charming harbour of Port Leone, modern Piraeus, disfigured though it was for him one day by the sight of a ship loading up with Lord Elgin's 'spoils'. But the tomb of Themistocles was said to be carved in one of these cliffs above Piraeus, and from the heights Byron could see across to the Parthenon in perspective, as if entire, and the Theseum in full glory.

What would Byron have thought of modern industrial Piraeus? One hopes he would have been consoled to see a Greek port thriving. The beauty of Athens' empty plain in 1809 meant poverty, while its present congestion with roads, houses and factories brings it in a sense nearer to the busy city of classical times, already spreading beyond its walls.

The daily rides of Byron and Hobhouse took them also to one or other of the three great mountains: Pentelicus, Hymettus and Parnes. Mt Pentelicus

ABOVE The view from the Kaisariani monastery on Mount Hymettus, which
Byron and Hobhouse visited during their daily rides from Athens.

has scarcely changed, at least from a distance, since the marble was quarried for the Parthenon and all its kindred temples on the Acropolis. Byron and Hobhouse saw the entrance to these caverns – two marble precipices overhung with ivy. Inside they found tombs, painted saints, travellers' *graffiti* (possibly their own were added), a spring and fantastic pillars 'with the drop trembling from the white icicle above towards the rising crystal below'. Even Hobby (as Byron called his friend) waxed poetical.

The monastery of Kaisariani on Mt Hymettus which the friends visited still stands. Hobhouse thought it stood on the site of an ancient Temple of Venus, for the monks showed them four ruined marble columns and a medicinal spring which Athenian matrons used to visit as a cure for sterility. The monks' information was correct, though they did not tell Hobhouse about the properties of the water. Byron reported a dearth of the celebrated honey, despite the abundance of thyme and myrtle growing wild on the mountain. (The ancient bees used the mines as their hives.)

Mt Parnes is a dream of beauty and wildness, particularly in the evening. For Byron, its memory was perhaps tarnished by that terrifying incident in its splendid cave, when the explorers as well as their guide got lost and saw daylight again only as the last torch was about to expire. Hobhouse could not picture a fate more terrible than 'slow sudden' death in a fairy palace which had been converted in one second into a tomb.

ABOVE RIGHT A rugged slope of Mount Parnes.

For us, Parnes may be blemished by the casino and radar on its crest. But nothing could be lovelier even now than its winding tracks, rising from heathland dotted with furze, juniper and drifts of wild orchids in every shade of purple, skirting one after another the deep ravines made mysterious by vapours or broken shafts of sunlight, and running beneath cliffs of violet and blue rock splashed with geometrical patterns of ochre, primrose and vermillion. When Byron rode on his horse or mule up Mt Parnes, it was green almost to the top with holly-oaks, firs and pines. From Parnes came the charcoal for Athenian fires. Corn was grown in some of the open glades and there were abundant hares, partridges, wolves and wild boars.

By the spring of 1810 Byron and Hobhouse together had explored almost all of Attica and many other places around. They saw the monastery at Daphne, named from the shrubs growing on the slopes of the mountain which Hobhouse called oleander. The mosaic figure of Christ on the cupola of the church struck them chiefly because the eyes had been perforated after a 'visitation' by the Turks.

They saw Eleusis, for centuries the scene of the thrilling and sinister 'Mysteries' initiated in honour of Demeter; now like Piraeus a growing industrial centre; in Byron's time a miserable hamlet of thirty mud huts inhabited by Albanians, who dug up ancient coins and sold them to travellers, (twenty-five to Hobhouse).

They saw ruined Megara, remarkable for two things: the women ground their corn on slabs of ancient marble, and had been drinking from a well dedicated to nymphs. It had made them 'incontinent', however, and their husbands had recently blocked it up.

They saw on a promontory above the island of Salamis the craggy 'throne' from which King Xerxes was supposed to have watched the decisive naval battle between his Persians and the Greeks in 481 BC. Byron celebrated the defeat of Xerxes in *Don Juan*:

> *A King sate on the rocky brow*
> > *Which looks o'er sea-born Salamis;*
> *And ships, by thousands, lay below,*
> > *And men in nations; – all were his!*
> *He counted them at break of day –*
> *And, when the Sun set, where were they?*

Only one expedition is recorded by Hobhouse, (to Euboea), when Byron was detained in Athens and could not accompany his friend. He was missed as a companion who united 'gay good humour' with 'quickness of observation and ingenuity of remark'.

At last the moment had come for the pilgrims to tear themselves away from this Athenian oasis and set forth again on their travels. Byron had long

A view of Salamis from Megara.

89

determined to cross the Aegean and see Constantinople and the East. There was possibly also another reason for a temporary break.

He may have decided to remove himself from the growing temptation of Theresa's charms, just as he may have left England partly because he felt his relations with Edleston could not remain for ever on their purely romantic level. The atmosphere in the Macris' house seems to have warmed up with the springtime, encouraging even the sexually diffident Hobhouse to try his luck with one of the girls – though without success. In Mrs Macri's mind the whole thing was probably cut and dried: an English lord – or any other man for that matter who fell in love with one of her daughters – either married the girl or paid a traditional sum for taking her away with him.

Byron, as we shall see, would never accept either of these alternatives. Instead, he was later to honour Katinka and Dudu by placing them in the harem visited by Don Juan. As for Theresa, she was to be immortalised in his 'Maid of Athens':

> *Maid of Athens, ere we part,*
> *Give, oh, give me back my heart!*

11 Turkey: 'My Grand Giro'

In his Turkish tale, *The Bride of Abydos*, Byron makes his hero Selim assure Zuleika that if they elope and wander the world together, they will find 'each clime hath charms'. Byron may have hoped to find that Turkey 'hath charms' comparable to those of Greece. If so, he was disappointed.

The three days' journey over the Aegean, where 'the purple of Ocean is deepest in dye', only increased his nostalgia for the Greece he was temporarily leaving behind him. (He and Hobhouse had galloped at full speed to Piraeus in order to cut short the pain of parting.) Smyrna (Izmir), where he arrived on 8 March 1810, could not offer him the novelty it produces for the modern traveller. Izmir may be our first experience of Turkish customs, bazaars, shrines and faces. But Byron had already seen all these things in Turkish-occupied Greece. Indeed, he consistently grouped Turkey, Albania and Greece together as forming 'the clime of the East', with Greece as its 'greenest Island'.

The drive from Smyrna to Ephesus did not reassure him. He found the countryside marshy and desolate. But at least his horse-drawn transport and kindly and philosophical Turkish guide, Suleiman, got him and Hobhouse to their destination in one piece. The same journey made soon after World War II by a far larger party of tourists including this writer entailed a fleet of buses gaily painted with flowers but one of them empty. A Turkish guide, no less kindly than Byron's Suleiman, refrained from explaining the reason for this 'loose horse'. It explained itself all too soon. One of the buses broke down and its passengers were philosophically transferred into the spare.

Ephesus disappointed Byron for a simple and understandable reason. As with all the ancient sites he visited, whether in Turkey, Albania or Greece, the great nineteenth- and twentieth-century archaeologists had not yet begun to unearth their fabulous treasures. Byron was inclined to take a lordly view of Ephesus, ignoring even such ruins as were visible. He preferred to raise his eyes to the hills and listen to the heart-broken cry of the jackals: 'I smoke and stare at mountains, and twirl my mustachios very independently, I miss no comforts, and the Musquïtoes that rack the morbid frame of Hobhouse, have ... little effect on mine because I live more temperately.' One would not like to assume, with Byron, that delicious local wine and dishes of *pilaff* (which incidentally the insular Fletcher could not eat) make modern travellers more attractive to blood-suckers than if they adopted a Byronic diet of boiled rice, vinegar and water. Nor should one assume that Ephesus, if Byron had seen it today, would not have impressed him even more than the jackals' night chorus.

Two Englishmen have since uncovered the site of the Temple of Artemis (Diana) – one of the 'Seven Wonders of the World' – and Byron could now

Mount Pentelicus seen from Melissa.

pace, musing, along 1700 feet of the splendidly paved Arcadian Way, flanked by the bases and shafts of marble pillars. In the acoustically miracu-lous Theatre where the silversmiths barracked St Paul ('Great is Diana of the Ephesians'), one could whisper the name 'Byron' and be heard on the furthest benches. Byron himself, however, remained invincibly cynical about Ephesus and its saints and sinners: 'St Paul need not trouble himself to epistolize the present brood of Ephesians who have converted a large church ... into a Mosque, and I don't know that the edifice looks the worst for it.'

It was the Amazons who were said to have founded Ephesus. Whether this would have endeared the city to Byron remains doubtful. A female soldier was no more his type than the 'female wit' he was soon to meet in Athens. But at least in Turkey the ideal of feminine beauty conformed closely to his own. Exquisitely rounded, resilient and devoted, there is not an unwomanly woman among his heroines – be it the 'gentle' Medora, 'soft' Gulnare, 'faithful' Kaled, 'fair' Leila, 'graceful' Zuleika, 'warm' Lolah, 'lovely' Katinka, 'languishing' Dudu, or innocent Haidée most perfect of all, with her 'little hand', 'small snow feet' and warbling voice 'low and sweet', whose father was Lambro the pirate.

About his own figure Byron seems to have been ambivalent. After a fever, as we shall see, he regretted the disappearance of 'plump', 'rounded' Byron as much as any Turkish pasha. At the same time he wanted to remain thin.

The high-water mark of Byron's four-month holiday in Turkey was the Hellespont. Here ancient and modern times met and fused in the way he always wished. Young Leander in legendary days had swum across the Hellespont every night from Abydos to Sestos, where his lover Hero awaited him in her tower. Now young Byron, on 3 May 1810, swam from Sestos to Abydos. His friends might smile at such an exploit, 'but as it made an ancient immortal, I see no reason', he wrote, 'why a modern may not be permitted to boast of it. . . .'

Without the incentive of a Hero, Byron nevertheless had an unusually excited Hobby to spur him on, not to mention the prospect of fame, which in fact produced many subsequent imitators. As Byron wrote in some verses six days after his exploit, Leander 'swum for Love, as I for Glory'. He described his success in all his letters home, but with his usual undertone of irony. To Henry Drury he wrote on the very afternoon of 3 May after his one hour and ten minutes in the sea. He was obviously still in a state of euphoria. 'This morning I *swam* from *Sestos* to *Abydos*, the immediate distance is not above a mile, but the current renders it hazardous, so much so, that I doubt whether Leander's conjugal powers must not have been exhausted in his passage to Paradise.' Byron's epistolatory powers were clearly not exhausted, for his letter was enormously long. Though he declared towards the end that he intended, on returning home, 'to snarl all my life' like Diogenes the Cynic, there was no sign that his snarl would be less high-spirited than his swim. Moreover, he 'trumpeted' the news of his 'feat' (his own words) not without cause.

The 'roaring Hellespont' whipped by a north wind, had been too rough for his first attempt a week earlier. He and his fellow swimmer, Lt William Eckenhead, had been so numbed after one hour in the water that they could not stand. Even when they succeeded, the current had forced them to beat up and down the channel for a total distance of four miles. Byron took seventy minutes, Eckenhead sixty-five. A print of the period shows that swimmers would be faced with a choppy sea and a harbour uncomfortably crowded with vessels scudding here, there and everywhere under full sail or caïques raising fountains of spray with their spiky oars.

For once, Byron seems to have been bothered while in the Dardanelles by the kind of historical problems which were generally left to Hobhouse. Homer had spoken of the 'boundless' or 'broad' Hellespont. Yet it was manifestly under a mile wide. Byron hit upon a characteristic solution. 'Probably Homer had the same notion of distance that a coquette has of time', he wrote; 'and when he talks of boundless means half a mile; as the latter . . . when she says *eternal* attachment, simply specifies three weeks.'

Homer again seemed to be in trouble when Byron and Hobhouse visited the plains of Troy. Did the barrows which they saw really 'contain the carcases' of the Greek heroes who had laid Troy waste? Byron was sceptical. 'The Troad is a fine field for conjecture and Snipe-shooting', he reflected. He lost his way 'in a cursed quagmire' of the River Scamander beside which Trojan Paris lay buried.

In Constantinople it was the famous city wall, second only to the Great Wall of China, which caught Byron's imagination. The total circuit was nearly twelve miles, punctuated by four hundred and fifty gates. Byron loved the ride of four miles on the landward side, and counted 218 towers. Beyond the huge, dark, ivied bastions were Turkish burying grounds – 'the loveliest spots on earth'. Byron's enthusiasms were never misplaced. A garden full of Turkish gravestones, each a simple *stele* covered with elegant characters from the Koran and crowned with a carved stone turban is indeed an innocently pretty sight. The 'huge cypresses' in the cemeteries were also beloved of Byron and must have made a striking contrast with the doll-like gravestones. Byron's glowing appreciation flowed out to embrace 'the prospect on each side from the Seven Towers to the end of the Golden Horn'. At the time, it impressed him more than the ruins of Ephesus, Delphi, and – yes – Athens.

But that was where his Turkish enthusiasm stopped. Unlike Ali Pasha, the Sultan paid no particular attention to Lord Byron's rank, scarlet jacket, gold epaulettes or, for that matter, small ears, little white hands and dark curls. (His naturally pale skin was described around this date as 'bronzed' and his chestnut-brown curls as 'auburn'.) He was received at the palace *after* Mr Stratford Canning, mere secretary of the British Embassy. He was a cousin of George Canning, then a politician under a cloud but destined to become a future British prime minister and gallant pro-Greek. Neither of these atoning facts could Byron foresee. And so, slighted by the Sultan and outstripped by a plain mister, he sulked in his tent like Achilles on the plains of Troy. Snobbish foibles apart, Byron's regrettable reaction was as much a result of nostalgic feeling for Ioannina as resentment against Constantinople.

Ioannina had been his first, delightful, strongly personalised experience of Turkish rule. His brain had told him that a cruel oppressor lurked behind Ali Pasha's white beard; but his eyes and his heart did not corroborate this intelligence. Since then, however, he had met Greek nationalists, heard Greek nationalist songs and travelled widely over Greece. He knew something of what it was to be a helot under the Sultan's sway. True, he had seen a man's arm hanging from a tree on his first day in Ioannina. But on his first day in Constantinople he had seen a whole human body being eaten by a dog and later on the horror was multiplied:

> And he saw the lean dogs beneath the wall
> Hold o'er the dead their carnival,
> Gorging and growling o'er carcass and limb;
> They were too busy to bark at him!

He felt no unwitting *tendresse* for the Sultan, such as he had felt for Ali. This was as it should be. In fourteen years' time he was to be fighting this same Sultan from Missolonghi.

As a parting thrust at Turkish prestige, he told his mother that St Sophia was not a patch on St Paul's, adding quickly, 'I speak like a *cockney*.' He certainly did not want to see St Paul's again for many a long month. But he did want Greece.

12 *The Peloponnese : 'Girating the Morea'*

Byron's growing involvement with Greece is shown by one of his epistolatory gimmicks. As long ago as November 1809 he had written to his agent, 'I have no intention or wish to return to your country. . . .' Five months later he was comparing for his mother's benefit the Trojan mounds to 'the barrows of Danes in your Island'; and from then on most of his correspondents would get a whiff of Byron's disenchantment with England and attachment to Greece. There were frequent, aloof references to 'your Country', 'your foggy Island', 'you *Northern Gentry*', interspersed with declarations to the effect that he himself was 'a citizen of the world'. Despite

Byron's genuine and increasing cosmopolitanism, however, his world citizenship was in reality mediated through Greece.

His knowledge of the wide world was romanticised in much the same way as he exaggerated his other achievements, not least the shocking ones. No doubt he intended eventually to visit India and Persia, but money was not forthcoming from his agent even for a preliminary trip to Jerusalem and Cairo. The wish was father to the thought when he listed Africa as among the continents he had seen – or perhaps he thought it was enough to have glimpsed its coast from the boat as he left Gibraltar. Spain itself he knew only sketchily in the south-west; Portugal the same. Turkey meant a little of the Anatolian coast plus the Dardanelles and Bosphorus. But Greece – ah, there was real understanding, real commitment. With justice he had written from Smyrna, 'I have traversed the greatest part of Greece besides Epirus &c. . . .' By the end of July 1810 he was making the same point in more significant language: 'The greater part of Greece is already my own. . . .'

The voyage back to Athens was remarkable for two things. He found a Turkish *ataghan* on deck and carefully examined its sharp blade and engraved sheath, entering as he did so into the feelings of a Turk about to stab an enemy to death. This was typical of Byron's developing interest in other people, especially their emotions. It was to emerge in his Eastern poems of blood and thunder, like the *Corsair, Lara, The Giaour, Bride of Abydos* and *Siege of Corinth*. His contemporaries found in these tales a modicum of fine poetry but ample substitutes for the romantic thrillers which bestride the market today. Byron seemed to know the human heart in its moments both of dramatic exposure and mystery – particularly mystery.

The second event was his parting from Hobhouse on the island of Zea (Keos) on 17 July. Hobhouse's travels were finished for the time being and he was off home. The two friends shared a bunch of wild flowers, each taking half. That might sound as if theirs was an *amitié amoureuse*. It was of course not so. But there was something else special for Byron in this friendship. Hobhouse was his 'Lala', a word Byron had first heard, as we know, on the lips of Ali Pasha's little grandson. Without a 'Lala' or moral tutor, it was not safe for young gentlemen like Lord Byron to travel around the world.

But 'Lalas' too often say Don't and No. For this reason, Byron was to feel a sense of liberation as well as loss when Hobhouse had departed. His 'Lala' was so 'very crabbed and disagreeable' that he could not but rejoice in the man's absence. Nevertheless – 'After all, I do love thee, Hobby, thou hast so many good qualities, and so many bad ones, it is impossible to live with or without thee.' There was something of the same ambivalence when Byron met the dutiful and governessy Annabella Milbanke. But in her case the tensions of sex were added, without Hobby's wit.

Hobhouse's feelings for Byron could be equally ambivalent. Because he was always changing his mind Byron was 'a difficult person to live with',

Hobhouse confessed, as if speaking of an awkward but fascinating charge. How impossible Byron could become when his 'Lala' had departed for good was to appear in many boisterous letters written to friends – Hobhouse included – over the next year.

Classical ruins at Mantinea.

Back in Athens on 19 July 1810, Byron found that another parting of friends had to be quickly effected. He had gone as before to the Macri lodgings. But he stayed for only one full day. Either he already suspected Mother Macri of designs upon his status of bachelor and his purse (the latter singularly empty owing to his agent's difficulties and dilatoriness) or he now became aware of a change in the atmosphere, destroying the Haidée-like innocence of Theresa and her sisters. Probably both were true. Byron arrived back prepared for a change, and Mother Macri had alerted her daughters to the dangers of English lodgers. Almost immediately – on 21 July – he set out for a grand tour of the Morea (Peloponnese). He did not lodge again with the Macris on returning to Athens in a month's time.

Meanwhile his grand tour of the Morea had become 'My Grand Giro', a commentary on the dizzy whirligig of this pilgrim's progress.

The Grand Giro suffers inevitably from Byron's dictum that all description is disgusting. Without descriptions of his own, and now without Hobhouse's supplementary journal, the weeks in the Morea flash by, filled with exciting sketches for events which never became finished paintings. We have hardly caught sight of the milestones on his journey – Corinth, Vostitza, Patras, Megara, Mantinea, Tripolitza – before he is off again on another preposterous adventure.

Byron began the tour with his old Cambridge friend Lord Sligo, but shook him off at Corinth. He was 'woefully sick of travelling companions', he had told his mother before starting. The only other information he imparted to her concerned his suite: 'two Turks, two Greeks, a Lutheran, and the Nondescript Fletcher'. It was more amusing to describe them by their religions than their names. The idea later went into verse as a possible prelude to his *Siege of Corinth*:

> *We were of all tongues and creeds; –*
> *Some were those who counted beads,*
> *Some of mosque, and some of church.*
> *And some, or I mis-day, of neither;*
> *Yet through the wide world might ye search,*
> *Nor find a motlier crew nor blither.*

On the 29th Hobhouse got a lively account of the first week: Sligo's two servants in *leather breeches* despite the thermometer standing at 125°, Sligo himself 'not very easy in his seat', Fletcher 'with his usual acuteness' contriving to 'ram his damned clumsy foot into a boiling teakettle' at Megara. In Corinth came the welcome separation from Lord Sligo. Here also had once lived Byron's favourite philosopher, Diogenes, who asked Alexander the Great to take his shadow off him.

> *The grass my table-cloth, in open air*
> *On Sunium or Hymettus, like Diogenes,*
> *Of whom half my philosophy the progeny is.*

And here stood, and still stands, the ancient Temple of Apollo – another of those noble ruins which irritated Byron instead of inspiring him.

There is a temple in ruins stands,
Fashioned by long forgotten hands;
Two or three columns, and many a stone,
Marble and granite, with grass o'ergrown! ...
Till Ruin makes the relics scarce,
Then Learning acts her solemn farce,
And, roaming through the marble waste,
Prates of beauty, art, and taste.

Nevertheless, Byron *was* inspired by Corinth, but by a later and bloodier moment in her chequered history – the Turkish siege of 1715, when the city was destroyed in a 'sounding battle' which echoed far beyond the Isthmus:

You might have heard it, on that day,
O'er Salamis and Megara ...
Even unto Piraeus' bay.

Byron was to dedicate his *Siege of Corinth* to Hobhouse, in 1816.

The two young peers having parted in Corinth, Sligo for Tripolitza (Tripolis), Byron for Patras, the next stop for the latter's party was Vostitza (Aigion) on 25 July. Here began a ridiculous but romantic adventure. 'Thus far the ridiculous part of my narrative belongs to others, now comes my turn,' wrote Byron endearingly to Hobhouse.

At Vostitza he found his 'dearly-beloved Eustathius', whom he and Hobhouse had first met during their previous visit. Eustathius Georgiou was a Greek boy, undoubtedly beautiful and probably illiterate. Byron had almost certainly planned his Grand Giro partly with Eustathius in mind, for he had written as long ago as May that he expected to pass the summer 'amongst my friends the Greeks of the Morea'. Eustathius was the friend who counted. Moreover, the boy himself had followed up an earlier invitation by begging Byron in April to let him join his suite when he resumed his travels in Greece.

Alas! the love of boys! The five-day romance was as ridiculous as Byron said. On the first day, Eustathius vowed to follow Byron to England or the ends of the earth. On the second, 'the dear soul' outraged Fletcher and astonished even Byron by cavorting on horseback 'with those ambrosial curls hanging down his amiable back' and in his hand a *parasol*. On the third, still 'very much enamoured', they reached the house of Consul Strané in Patras, with whom Byron had business. On the fourth, the boy visited an 'accursed cousin' who must have said something to provoke the 'grand quarrel' which ended the honeymoon of Byron and Eustathius on the fifth day.

Consul Strané accused Byron of spoiling the boy and Byron admitted he was as 'froward as an unbroken colt'. After a threatened parting there was a temporary reconciliation but not before milord had submitted to a deluge of tears and 'as many kisses as would have sufficed for a boarding-school'; in

The ruins of old Corinth.

return, Byron presented the excitable youth with sal volatile and exchanged his 'effeminate' parasol for a more sober green shade.

Byron's rueful judgement on this affair was to apply equally well, but far more poignantly to the last boy-love of his life. 'I think I never in my life took so much pains to please anyone, or succeeded so ill.'

Early in August, Byron decided to visit Veli Pasha at Tripolitza, the fortified capital of the Turkish governor of the Morea. He travelled by way of Mantinea, where Epaminondas had been killed in battle. Veli was Ali's son and little Mahmout's father. Byron described the very embarrassing interview between himself and Veli in two letters to Hobhouse, the second after he had arrived safely back in Athens. 'I have girated the Morea and was presented with a very fine horse (a stallion) and honoured with a number of squeezes and speeches by Velly Pacha. . . .' It may have been Veli's squeezings, conducted shamelessly 'in *public*', which irretrievably upset the jealous page, Eustathius, and brought on an epileptic fit. For Byron's 'amiable' boy was apparently subject to fits. He had been 'prancing' by his side as far as Tripolitza, but from there was sent home to his father.

Having 'girated' the Morea, taking in Argos and Nauplia (but missing out unexcavated Mycenae), Byron re-established himself in Athens. A letter to Hobhouse dated 23 August gave his new address as 'The Convent'. From this seemingly pious base, Byron was to inaugurate another period of frenzied but entertaining follies.

13   *Athens : Drama at Piraeus*

'If I am a poet,' Byron was to tell Trelawny, 'the air of Greece has made me one.' The air of Greece can still work wonders, perhaps even turning new generations of tourists into lyricists. In Byron's case it had already produced two cantos of *Childe Harold*; and many intoxicating eastern tales were fermenting in his imagination. But that champagne air was to make Byron much else besides a poet. A lover, philanderer, reveller, student and unsatiable wanderer over her lovely landscape.

His next romantic attachment had already been indicated to Hobhouse from Tripolitza. Having written, 'I have sent Eustathius home . . .', Byron followed this news with the remark: 'You remember Nicolo at Athens Lusieri's wife's brother . . .' Hobhouse would have taken the hint. It happened that fifteen-year-old Nicolo Giraud was one of six pupils presently at school in the Capuchin convent (in fact monastery) of Athens, which took in the sons of Frankish families as boarders, while also offering accommodation to travellers in a city which had no inns. To this commodious building Byron removed himself and his suite, after Mother Macri put down her conventional Greek foot.

Byron gave away his excitement at being under the same roof as Nicolo when he tried to list for Hobhouse the six pupils by name: three he remembered, two he forgot – but Nicolo's name was underlined. This charming and accomplished French boy was Lusieri's brother-in-law as Byron said. Just as Eustathius had been teaching Byron Romaic or modern Greek, Nicolo would teach him Italian, which from now on was to bespatter his letters.

A view across the Agora
to the Acropolis.

All this was only one of the convent's attractions. Among the Italian words
which Byron had learned was *ragazzi* – boys – and this is how he referred to
the six lively pupils of the genial abbot. From dawn to dusk they would keep
up the dizzy pace, shouting to Byron to come downstairs – *venite abasso* – in
the early morning (not generally his forte) and indulging in 'scamperings',
'waggeries', 'eating fruit and peltings and playings' until he felt that these
imps, sylphs, lads or even gentlemen (as he variously called them) had carried
him back to his own youth. The Albanian washerwomen in the 'giardino'

were not unaffected by the spirits of this convent school, since they spent their coffee-breaks 'in running pins into Fletcher's backside'. Nor did Byron's suite fail to contribute in their own way. They became 'very disorderly', 'very obstreperous' and drank 'skinfuls of Zean wine at 8 paras the oke daily', while nightly three of them (one being Fletcher) romped with their mistresses and two more were 'fooling with Dudu Roque and Mariana Macri'. But presumably the two mamas prevented these 'amours' from going any further. And the well-protected Theresa seems for the time to have quite lost Byron – 'I have better amusement', he boasted. There was in fact another girl with 'beautiful black eyes and raven locks' whom he was pursuing. *'Vive l'Amour!'*

The monument of Lysikrates, built *c.* 334 BC is all that remains of the Capuchin convent in which Byron lived in Athens. The monument had been incorporated into the convent courtyard and was used as a library by the poet.

At its most innocent the atmosphere was a reversion to his schooldays. 'I am vastly happy and childish,' he told Hobby, 'and shall have a world of anecdotes for you. . . .' He was back at Harrow-on-the-Hill, except that he was now under the Hill, and the Hill was Athena's.

The romantic position of the Capuchin convent under the Acropolis added to its charm: 'I am living in the Capuchin convent,' wrote Byron with true exhilaration, 'Hymettus before me, the Acropolis behind, the Temple of Jove to my right, the Stadium in front, the town to the left; eh, Sir, there's a situation, there's your picturesque!' The convent stood on the site of the present small public garden majestically overshadowed by the east face of the Acropolis. The old Acropolis walls around the summit of the perpendicular cliff, which Byron saw every morning, have been replaced by a later wall. Otherwise, we see the east face today as Byron saw it and feel no surprise that he was happy here. A few steps around the corner and he was opposite the vast south face, the foreground clothed with evergreens and wild weeds as it is today. Curiously enough, it is just behind the convent site that some of the narrow streets and small houses of old Athens – Byron's Athens – also remain.

By far the most striking relic of Byron's last home in Athens is the tall, circular Monument of Lysikrates, dating from 334 BC. Originally this build-ing had been erected as a thank-offering to the god Dionysus in what was then the Street of Tripods. Lysikrates of Kikina had won a drama contest with a chorus of boys. Some time in the eighteenth or late seventeenth century the Monument was incorporated into the courtyard of the Capuchin convent as its library, and called the 'Lantern of Demosthenes' in the mistaken belief that the ancient orator had prepared his political thunders within its hollow drum-like walls.

When Byron arrived he found that the Monument was being used as a dormitory for Giuseppe, one of the boarders, but it was apparently restored to its former use as a library, for the poet. He sat in the diminutive circular recess of the Monument's upper storey, a green cloth curtain dividing him from the rest of the convent. It was said that here Padre Paolo introduced him to the Greek 'underground'.

Stone from Piraeus and marble from Hymettus, Pentelicus and Eleusis combine to give the old library a mellow glow, in contrast to the dark granite background of the Acropolis. Its six monolithic Corinthian columns remain in a ring around the drum to support the tripod, which has vanished. During the War of Independence the convent was unluckily burned down, but the Monument was saved. On its frieze we can see Dionysus turning some tiresome pirates into dolphins – an art which might have served Byron at Sounion if the Maniots had proved less cautious, or even come in useful when the 'scamperings' of the *ragazzi* outside the library became unendurable.

Byron Street (written *Vironos*) today leads up from the wide Areopagitou thoroughfare to the Monument of Lysikrates, a street of shops and old nineteenth-century houses with balconies, much like Byron Street in Ioannina. Almost at right angles to Vironos Street, Lissikratous Street runs straight down to the Arch of Hadrian. You can still see the Arch from the Monument, just as Byron saw it; and despite an ugly web of overhead wires of one sort or another above the street, Mt Hymettus still glimmers violet in the distance.

The twin inscriptions on Hadrian's Arch, the earlier one Greek and the later one Roman, marked the boundary between Greek and Roman Athens. On the side of the Arch facing Byron and his convent it said: 'This is Athens, the ancient city of Theseus'. With its back to him, however, a higher storey of the Arch dared to proclaim: 'This is the city of Hadrian and not of Theseus'. Now it was the city of Sultan Mahmud 11 – but not for long.

Byron's rides to Piraeus had become a daily event. He would swim for an hour, usually right across the bay, wearing trunks like the modest Turks instead of plunging in naked like the Greeks. Afterwards he would indulge in a reverie on some lonely rock, with the faithful and unobtrusive Nicolo in attendance. Hobhouse, of course, would have frowned upon this idyll.

Moreover, he and Hobhouse would have 'wrangled', as they used to wrangle every day, on how best to spend one's time abroad. Hobhouse would 'potter with map and compass' at the foot of every mountain, greedy for 'legendary lore, topography, inscriptions'. Byron rode his mule up the mountains. 'They had haunted my dreams from boyhood; the pines, eagles, vultures, and owls were descended from those Themistocles and Alexander had seen, and were not degenerated like the humans; the rocks and torrents the same. . . . I gazed at the stars and ruminated; took no notes, asked no questions.' A poet must necessarily stand and stare at Pindus, Parnes, and Parnassus as Byron did, or sit and gaze at the isles of Greece from above Piraeus. The rest of us must be at least part Hobhouses, taking notes and asking questions. What a 'delightful companion' Hobby was in retrospect, now that he had gone home!

Slightly to Byron's left, out there in the middle of the Saronic Gulf, was the island of Aegina, whose fleet had once fought so gallantly in the decisive naval battle against the Persians at Salamis, close in on his right.

> *Descending fast the mountain shadows kiss*
> *Thy glorious gulf, unconquered Salamis!*

Today instead of triremes a fleet of red-sailed fishing vessels appears at evening between the gleaming mainland and the deep blue silhouette of Salamis.

One day in September 1810 the deep peace of Piraeus was brutally violated. An armed guard had been noticed by Byron escorting a sinister cortege to the seashore, just as he had left it. Something told him to question these people. His servant brought back the news that a Turkish girl had been taken in adultery. But instead of saying to her, 'Go and sin no more', the Turkish governor of Athens had had her sewn in a sack. She was carried down to Piraeus and was now about to be drowned.

This was a dreadful reincarnation of Kyra Frossyni at Ioannina; but here the Kyra had indeed sinned, and probably sinned with Byron. Without doubt Byron knew the girl. She may even have been, as Professor Marchand suggests, the dark-eyed raven-haired beauty whom Byron had been pursuing a few weeks earlier. Overcome with horror, he contrived to stay her execution and get her sentence transmuted from death to exile. She was hidden in the Capuchin convent until nightfall, when he smuggled her over the Attic border into Boeotia. But if the Kyra was safe, Byron was far from sound. His heart and mind had been seized in an 'icy' grip, never completely forgotten. To some extent, however, he did exorcise the horror by writing his poem *The Giaour*. The nameless hero-villain, a 'giaour' or Christian infidel, is loved by Leila, Turkish Hassan's favourite slave. Her secret is discovered and she suffers the traditional fate on the sea-shore –

> *Sullen it plunged, and slowly sank,*
> *The calm wave rippled to the bank. . . .*

It was the same fate which Gulnare in *The Corsair* dreaded:

> *There yawns the sack – and yonder rolls the sea –*

The guilt-tortured Giaour is seen for an instant by a fisherman thundering along the stand of Piraeus:

> *But in that instant o'er his soul*
> *Winters of Memory seemed to roll,*
> *And gather in that drop of time,*
> *A life of pain, an age of crime.*

The Giaour has caused Leila's horrible death and also treacherously murdered Hassan in revenge. Did Byron, who had recently run his finger along the blade of an ataghan, wondering what it felt like to commit murder, even contemplate murdering the Governor of Athens, had he proved adamant? We shall never know. Byron was mysterious about the whole episode, bound, like the Gaiour, by 'a nameless spell'.

A few days' later, who should see Lord Byron diving off the mole of Piraeus but Lady Hester Stanhope. This eccentric and redoubtable niece of the Younger Pitt, shared Byron's passion for travel in Eastern climes. It was the only thing she had in common with him. 'I think he has a strange character,' she said: 'a sort of Don Quixote, fighting with the police for a woman of the town. . . .' He was generous and avaricious, mopish and jocular by turns. But what could you expect of a man with 'so much vice in his looks', such contracted brows and eyes so close together? Only the curve of his neck and the curls on his forehead pleased her. He wanted to make himself 'something great'. Well, poetry was not the way to fame: 'It is easy enough to write verses.'

It was also easy enough, thought Byron, to crack malicious jokes. 'I saw Lady Hesther Stanhope at Athens,' he told Hobhouse, 'and do not admire "that dangerous thing a female wit".'

A final scene in the Piraeus drama took place when Lady Hester's lover, Michael Bruce, was about to leave Greece. This Bruce was a gallant and gay dog. In five or six years' time he would be having an affair with Byron's ex-mistress Lady Caroline Lamb in Paris, besides helping a French Bonapartist general to escape from the clutches of Louis XVIII and Wellington. Meanwhile Bruce stood at the end of the mole saying goodbye to Byron. Later, when Byron himself was sailing home from Greece, he wrote an account for Hobhouse of Bruce's surprising behaviour on that occasion. It was night-time: 'He made a profession of friendship, on the extremity of the Piraeus, the only one I ever received in my life, and certainly very unexpected, for I had done nothing to deserve it.'

Lady Hester Stanhope, the 'female wit', may have been responsible, as Professor Marchand suggests, for Byron's leaving Athens soon after her arrival. Certainly her residence in the Lebanon later on seems to have kept him out. 'He said he would have gone there,' reported Trelawny, 'if she had not forestalled him.'

At any rate, Byron was on the mole of the Piraeus again in mid-September. He planned a second 'Giro' of the Morea – his last.

14 'Most Social and Fantastical'

Towards the end of 1819 the poet Keats was looking at the meadows of Winchester and apostrophising the 'season of mists and mellow fruitfulness'. Byron, out in the Peloponnese, had found the autumn of 1810 a season of gales and malignant fevers. The first part of his tour, a storm-tossed voyage from the Piraeus to the Isthmus of Corinth was interrupted by his making the wrong landfall.

> Pronounce what sea, what shore is this?
> The Gulf, the rock of Salamis!

From Salamis, where he had been 'blown ashore', he put to sea again and then proceeded overland to Olympia, the only successful part of this tour.

For a thousand years the Olympic Games and Olympic Truce had been celebrated, with all their associations of friendly rivalry and peace between

The entrance to the stadium at Olympia.

Sheep and goats in the Peloponnese, on the road to Olympia.

Greek states. But there were no games in Byron's day. They had been suppressed by the Byzantine Emperor Theodosius I in AD 393, as a pagan festival. Nor were the games restarted until 1896, some twenty years after German excavators had begun uncovering the sacred precinct. Thus Byron, as usual, happened to visit some of the greatest of Greek treasures at a singularly obscure period in their history. True, the famous Dr Chandler had arrived on the site in 1766, the first modern traveller to visit Olympia with his eye on possible excavations. As one would expect, Byron made fun of him. And the year after Byron's visit (1811) the scholarly Lord Stanhope, relative of the 'female wit', mapped out the precinct. Neither Stanhope's name nor his activity were calculated to impress Byron.

His own limited sightseeing at Olympia would have seemed quite adequate, particularly as he was sickening for the prevalent fever. He would have seen the usual chaos of marble, and traces, perhaps, of race-grounds and of the two great temples of Zeus and Hera. But more important to Byron, Olympia was in a fertile valley shaded by pines and planes, with a pretty stone bridge over the quiet river. Here one could gaze and ruminate. One could even hear bird-song, a somewhat rare thing in Greece. The present museum, with its sensuous Hermes, lordly Apollo, battling Lapiths and labouring Heracles only enhances the essential peacefulness of the place. A kingfisher flashes under the bridge in spring.

As for the Olympic Games, one would like to imagine Byron swimming for Britain.

When Byron reached Patras the fever had got a firm hold on him. He was dosed with 'Bark' (quinine), a drug which he tended to equate with imminent dissolution. During the last period of his life he was expressing a wish to die as a soldier rather than relegated to bed and the bark. In fact it was to be the bark not the battle. But meanwhile in 1810 he recovered from the doses and purges of his physician, Dr Romanelli, though not without one relapse, three days in bed and four lines of verse in which Dr Romanelli was lampooned as having successfully extinguished his patient.

> *Youth, Nature and relenting Jove*
> *To keep my lamp in strongly strove,*
> *But Romanelli was so stout*
> *He beat all three – and blew it out.*

Byron's recovery was followed by the collapse of his beloved Nicolo, his only companion on the trip. After nursing Byron devotedly, Nicolo went down with the same fever. It was 13 October before the pair were safely back again in the Capuchin convent.

The fever had reduced Byron to remarkable slimness and he was determined to remain in that elegant state. To be sure, he had seemed on his sick-bed to lament the loss of his curves:

Poor B—r—n sweats – alas! how changed from him
So plump in feature, and so round in limb. . . .

Nevertheless, he continued with a rigorous diet in order to avoid regaining his lost weight. But when it came to lost time, Byron was soon making it up in a whirl of dissipation – 'fooleries with the females of Athens' – almost more debilitating than the fever itself. After the debauches there would be bouts of boredom: 'for my life has, with the exception of a very few moments, never been anything but a *yawn*.'

There was one group of friends who none the less lent meaning as well as spice to Byron's life. These were foreign scholars and archaeologists of some distinction, including a Dane and several Germans. How odd that scholars belonging to a profession which Byron affected to despise should have been the chief source of his latter-day contentment in Athens. It only went to show that some of his jibes could not be taken too seriously.

To this group of foreign visitors were added Monsieur Fauvel the French Consul and Signor Lusieri, Nicolo's brother-in-law. Byron was indeed happiest as a 'citizen of the world'. His winter in Athens had been 'most social and fantastical' – surely the perfect holiday recipe for any and every age.

But with the spring of 1811 his charmed circle began to melt away, many of its members resuming their travels. Byron was left more and more with the English, the women of the town – and a variety of diseases. 'I have a number of Greek and Turkish women, and I believe the rest of the English were equally lucky, for we were all *clapped*.' Byron himself added a cough, catarrh, piles, and pains in his side to the list of his penances.

By March 1811 the die was cast. He himself would leave Greece – on 22 April as it happened; thirteen years and three days before he was to leave not only Greece again, but the world. Despite his rejection of England ('*your* country', '*your* island') in so many letters, there were other letters where he clearly wanted to rejoin his English friends. 'I look forward to meeting you at Newstead,' he had written to Hobhouse, 'and renewing our old Champagne evenings. . . .' In any case, there was no money in the kitty for Asia, Africa, or perhaps even for keeping up Newstead. His repeated asseverations to his agent that he would *not* sell Newstead whatever happened, proved how fearful he was lest this very disaster should befall. 'I will not sell Newstead, *No*, *oXi*, *yok*, *yeo* (Albanesico) *Noah*, (Nottinghamshirico)' followed by two forms of No in Greek. Newstead was finally sold in 1817 for £94,500.

On 22 May in Malta he was gloomily jotting down a list of ugly facts which would become more intolerable as he grew older, unless he brought about a radical change in his life. 1. 'At twenty-three the best of life is over and its bitters double.' 2. 'I have seen Mankind in various Countries and found them equally despicable,' though the Turks less so. 3. 'I am sick at heart.' 4. 'A man who is lame of one leg is in a state of bodily inferiority which increases with years . . . in another existence I expect to have *two* if not *four* legs by way

Mountains north of Olympia on Byron's road to Patras.

of compensation.' Points 5, 6 and 7 amounted to a feeling that he had out-lived love and authorship, while his finances still failed miserably to live up to his hopes.

If these were his negative thoughts, his positive interests were exemplified by the trophies which he was bringing home with him. They included four live Athenian tortoises; a greyhound which died on the voyage to England; a golden serpent-ring with a spot of poison between its teeth; four ancient Athenian skulls; and a phial of Attic hemlock gathered by Byron outside the city walls, though Lusieri told him 'it dont poison people nowadays'. There were also locks of hair contributed by Nicolo Giraud, the three Maids of Athens and the Girl of Cadiz, some antique marbles which Hobhouse had asked Byron to transport for him and a silver funerary urn filled with bones.

Among all these objects, most of them inanimate or morbid, one radiant living form was conspicuously absent from his baggage. Theresa Macri, *the* Maid of Athens, had finally been offered to Byron by her mother for 30,000 piastres. He could not afford her; any more than he could afford the pleasure and responsibility of owning either Marathon, which had also been offered to him for a very reasonable sum, or Ithaca which he had thought of buying. All these lovely things had been left behind in Greece and only one of them – Ithaca – was he destined ever to see again.

The presence of Constance Spencer Smith in Malta no longer pleased him enough to compensate for the climate of 'this infernal oven', or the fever which again flared up, or the parting from Nicolo Giraud. Byron left a large sum for Nicolo's education. Gales and fog made the voyage home more tedious than expected. But at last he landed at Sheerness in Kent, thus completing a 'pilgrimage' of two years and twelve days. The date was 14 July – *le quatorze juillet* – the date of the storming of the Bastille twenty-two years before. It was not an inappropriate date. For Byron was arriving as a social and literary revolutionary to take London by storm.

Part II

PILGRIM OF ETERNITY

1 *England: The Famous Awakening*

By all accounts London in 1812 was absurdly gay. It was the Year of the Waltz. The lame Byron watched this 'duty free' German import from the sidelines, sardonically dubbing it the dance of Belial. To him it was not the Year of the Waltz so much as the year when he 'awoke and found himself famous'.

There had been a preliminary fanfare of publicity in February for his maiden speech as a peer defending the stocking-frame breakers of Nottingham. But it was with the publication of *Childe Harold* in March that Byron leapt into fame. This was a sudden reversal of the melancholy welcome he had received on arrival in England: four beloved figures, including his mother and Edleston, all dead. A sense of loneliness suddenly smote him:

> *Though pleasure fires the maddening soul,*
> *The heart – the heart is lonely still!*

After the publication of *Childe Harold*, London ballrooms tingled with the hopes of those aspiring to bring 'Childe Harold's' loneliness to an end. Lady Caroline Lamb was the first aspirant. She gave Byron hours of irritation for every minute of ecstasy – and Byron was to put a duration of sixteen minutes at most to any experience of happiness. On first seeing him she had summed him up in her diary as 'mad, bad, and dangerous to know.' It was sad for both of them that she insisted on knowing him. How could he escape from her?

Lady Melbourne, Caroline's mother-in-law and Byron's Delphic oracle, encouraged him to propose to her niece, Annabella Milbanke, who was an heiress. Byron called her his 'Princess of Parallelograms' because of her mathematical talent. He proposed, only to be rebuffed. But meanwhile Caroline had been superseded by Lady Oxford, whose 'autumnal charms' were both serene and glowing. For some reason, however, there was a breach, into which stepped his ill-fated half-sister, Mrs Augusta Leigh.

Sharing the family shyness with strangers and ease with one another, Byron and Augusta passed from comfortable familiarity to passion. They became lovers. Priestess Melbourne, consulted as usual by Byron, was horrified to hear of incest, a sin which did indeed shock as well as excite the sinner himself.

How could he be rescued from Augusta? A brief, unconsummated affair with the pallid and pious Lady Frances Wedderburn-Webster was no substitute for the real thing. Lady Melbourne sniffed the laurel leaves again and approved the same solution as before – Annabella Milbanke.

Byron's own laurels were luxuriant, as more and more poems issued from John Murray's publishing house. London was besotted with the Byronic

PREVIOUS PAGE
Byron in Albanian costume painted by Thomas Phillips.

Augusta Leigh,
from a drawing by
Sir George Hayter.

hero, both on paper and in the pale romantic flesh. *'That beautiful pale face is my fate,'* Caroline had written in her diary. The poet's skin looked paler than ever these days, since the auburn curls had turned dark brown under hair oil.

Byron's self-portrait in *Childe Harold* had established once for all the romantic type. It had to be 'dark' both in appearance and character, with a distinct touch of Lucifer; gifted with sensibility and devoted to sensation; impulsive, .violent, contrary, bored, satirical, arrogant, mysterious, in short 'Byronic' –

The wandering outlaw of his own dark mind.

Successive Byronic heroes added new romantic brush-strokes to the well-defined image. There was the Giaour (1812–13), the Corsair (1813), Lara (1814). And those who were in the know could see Byron's personal dilemma exposed in his portrait of Parisina (1816) and elsewhere. The incestuous Lady Parisina of Ferrara died because of 'that dark love she dared to feel'.

As yet there was no blue-print for Annabella Milbanke in Byron's poetry. This was not to appear until many years later, in *Don Juan*, where 'Donna Inez' is portrayed as unbearably virtuous: 'Oh! she was perfect past all parallel.' But one point about himself and the Princess of Parallelograms was clear almost from the start: their parallel lines must never meet. They were incompatible. Their union, he had said when she first turned him down, would have been 'but a *cold collation*, and I prefer hot suppers.'

Nevertheless the parallel lines did meet. For there were two overriding necessities in Byron's life: a substitute for Augusta and an heiress to repair his shattered fortune. Annabella seemed to offer both. Byron had awakened in March 1812 to find himself famous. He awoke in January 1815 to find himself married. It was a calamitous awakening.

They spent the honeymoon, or 'treaclemoon' as Byron called it, at Halnaby Hall in Yorkshire, a handsome eighteenth-century mansion with balustrades around roof and terrace and elegant plaster-work in the dining-room. But we shall never see where the Byrons dined and slept, for Halnaby Hall was one of the country houses destroyed – in 1952. The dining-room, however, with its ceiling and chandeliers, was salvaged and incorporated into a Yorkshire road-house.

Byron awoke to see flames from the sea-coal fire flickering on the red curtains of their four-poster bed. He imagined himself in Hell with Proserpina by his side. He was soon taunting Annabella with Augusta's superior charms. But when Augusta came to stay with them in their London home at 13 Piccadilly Terrace, he lashed out at both the women.

Byron was heading for a breakdown. Hounded by bailiffs, he resorted to heavy drinking and the Drury Lane Theatre, where all was 'hiccough and happiness'. With his daughter Ada's birth on 10 December 1815, his savage and alcoholic outbursts against Annabella, punctuated by suicidal depression, in no way abated.

The crack-up came on 3 January 1816. Byron decided to shut No. 13 and recklessly advised Annabella to take herself and Ada off to Yorkshire. His wife and child left on the 15th. They never returned to him. At first bewildered, he finally had to accept the harsh truth. Annabella had begun by believing he was mad. When her doctor ruled this out, she could only conclude he was bad. Caroline Lamb had confirmed Annabella's suspicions about Byron's relationship with Augusta.

A legal separation was completed on 21 April. Byron felt that the affair had turned all London against him – except a few gallant friends like Lady Jersey, Hobhouse and Leigh Hunt, editor of *The Examiner*. And of course, Claire Clairmont. This clever young 'drop-out', half-sister of Mary Godwin, the poet Shelley's future wife, had offered Byron consolation in a dark hour and inveigled him into seducing her on 16 April.

Eight days later, Byron was stretching himself on a grave – a favourite pastime – at Dover, while he waited for the packet to carry him away next day into exile. The grave was that of Charles Churchill, a satirical eighteenth-century poet who had 'blazed' for a season like a comet and then died, leaving behind – what?

> *The Glory and the Nothing of a Name.*

As he sailed on 25 April, Byron noticed something odd about Britain's receding coastline:

> *I recollect Great Britain's coast looks white,*
> *But almost every other country's blue. . . .*

To him, it was a whited sepulchre of cruelty and cant which he left behind for ever.

2 Italy : 'Paradise of Exiles'

Byron chose to see himself as 'self-exiled' a second time, rather than hounded out.

> *Self-exiled Harold wanders forth again.*
> *With naught of hope left but with less of gloom.*

Dr Polidori, his young secretary, noted how swiftly he was back in form the moment he had crossed the Channel. 'As soon as he reached his hotel room, Lord Byron fell like a thunderbolt upon the chambermaid.'

He explored the battlefield of Waterloo at a gallop, singing Albanian riding songs. Gliding down the 'fair Rhine', however, he was overwhelmed with remorse for the misery he had caused Augusta. Annabella's rejection of him still rankled; and what of Ada, 'Ada! sole daughter of my house and heart?' She was the 'child of love' though 'nurtured in convulsion'. Byron was not to recover easily from these convulsions.

But by a fortunate chance, his journey into the rarified glitter of the Swiss Alps was to prepare him for the next great influence on his life – Percy Bysshe Shelley.

The meeting of the two shy poets, Shelley and Byron, on the shores of Lake Geneva is one of history's seminal encounters. Under Shelley's inspiration, Byron's poetry soared into new regions. Sailing over the blue waters of Lake Geneva in Shelley's boat, they visited together the Castle of Chillon, where Byron, as at Sounion, first carved his name and then broke into poetry. Chillon had held prisoner the Swiss politician, Francois de Bonnivard. Byron also felt a prisoner of prejudice. Shelley 'dosed' Byron with Wordsworth, inducing in his friend an unlikely mood of nature-worship, so that Byron was soon submitting himself to the 'eternal harmony' of thunder, crags, cataract, avalanche and lake. He dared to equate his own defiance of society with Cain's, to challenge his Creator, and to pose the romantic's whole dilemma in one brief line of verse:

Great is their love who love in sin and fear.

Unlike Byron, Claire Clairmont knew nothing of sin or fear, but was pathetically determined to share a great love with a great poet, by whom incidentally she was pregnant. Claire, her half-sister Mary Godwin and *her* great poet had been waiting for Byron at the town of Geneva. Byron settled down in the Villa Diodati, within a few minutes' walk of the other three.

Geneva, as Mary was later to say of Pisa, had become a 'little nest of singing-birds', the two small households discussing poetry and metaphysics, telling ghost stories by candlelight, and scribbling away with the women acting as amanuenses. Inspired by a spooky session, Mary wrote the horror story, *Frankenstein*.

When Byron learnt of Claire's pregnancy, however, he cut her out of his life altogether. From his point of view, one compassionate step by him, and the whole disastrous cycle would have reopened. He had never loved her – 'but I could not exactly play the Stoic with a woman who had scrambled eight hundred miles to unphilosophize me. . . .' He agreed to acknowledge and bring up his child by Claire, but not to see the mother.

At the end of August the nest was vacated. Shelley took Mary and Claire home, Claire to give birth to Allegra on 12 January 1817. Meanwhile Byron, once again accompanied by his good friend Hobhouse, had set out across the Alps on 5 October 1816, into that country which, after Greece, contained 'the greenest island' of his imagination – Venice.

Childe Harold was ready to sing a new song, to make yet another lament. 'Italia! oh Italia!'

Byron's stay in Italy was to last from October 1816 to August 1823, so that he and Greece waited for one another, like Jacob and Rachel, for seven years.

His Italian period can be divided into two parts: before and after he fell in love with Countess Teresa Guiccioli in April 1819. Alternatively, one can put the dividing line a little earlier: before and after Byron became 'Don Juan', from having been 'Childe Harold' for so long. As the Don, Byron now applied himself to the business of living with cynicism and irony, laughter and relish, scorn and disgust. Deliberately abandoning the mysterious quality which had been the hallmark of *Childe Harold*, he wrote:

> *I hate all mystery, and that air*
> *Of clap-trap. . . .'*

This retreat from romantic melancholy in poetry was at first matched by flight from love to lust in real life. If he could not have Augusta, he would sate himself with gay, amusing, frankly animal, black-eyed Venetian prostitutes and peasants. The exhausting routine would consist of love-making far into the night and writing far into the small hours of morning. Though Hobhouse insistently summoned him to Rome for a spell of sight-seeing, Byron was at first too worn out with cuckoldry and composition to accept:

> *So we'll go no more a-roving*
> *So late into the night,*
> *Though the heart is as still as loving,*
> *And the moon be still as bright. . . .*

Byron's heart was indeed 'still as loving', and he was soon to meet in Venice the object of his 'last attachment': the nineteen-year-old wife of an Italian count three times her age – Teresa Gamba, married for just over a year to Count Guiccioli. 'I like the darkness of their gondolas', Byron had written, 'And the silence of their canals'. Within a week of their meeting Teresa's gondola was tying up regularly outside the Palazzo Mocenigo, Byron's splendid palace on the Grand Canal. Today there is a plaque on its wall placed there to mark, not so much Teresa's visits as Byron's fame, and his resolve that Venice should again be free.

When Teresa's husband swept her off to Ravenna, Byron followed. A second move, to Bologna, again found Byron in attendance. By 1820 Count Guiccioli had agreed to rent the upper floor of his palazzo in Ravenna to Teresa's lover.

Teresa Guiccioli brought to Byron three good gifts, and one which he could have done without. This last was the traditional Italian position of *cavalier servente*, a kind of permanent 'groomsman' who carried the fan and shawl for the wife, instead of merely the ring at the wedding for the husband. Both husband and wife were in theory his friends, while the wife was in

Teresa Guiccioli drawn
by Thomas d'Orsay.

practice his mistress. Such a state of artificial 'servitude' was not at all to Byron's taste. He preferred the Eastern (harem) system to the Italian, for 'here the *polygamy* is all on the female side'. Nevertheless, if he had outlived Count Guiccioli he might have made Teresa his wife and been happy. For he truly loved her. She brought him a golden beauty, a cultured intelligence and a congenial political circle among the Gambas.

The Gambas, father (Ruggero) and son (Pietro), were patriots after Byron's own heart. Through them he joined the revolutionary Carbonari, hailing the cause of Italy's liberation from Austria as 'the very *poetry* of politics'. The combination of this new political interest and Teresa's tears prevented him from following up an idea of returning to England or emigrating to America.

Meanwhile the three-cornered menage in the Palazzo Guiccioli in Ravenna had broken up. Provided Teresa lived under her father's roof (and not Byron's) she was granted a Papal separation from her husband in July 1820. Exactly a year after the separation the Gambas found themselves political exiles, banished from the Romagna. It was primarily a blow against Byron, the subversive poet whose published cantos of *Don Juan* had created such havoc in literary Britain. Teresa persuaded him to discontinue them temporarily. The government of Romagna expected Byron eventually to follow his lady, and indeed Byron's position on the second floor of the Palazzo Guiccioli was becoming more and more anomalous. He was virtually alone with his menagerie, which occupied most of the garden, staircase and ground floor of the Palazzo Guiccioli: eight huge dogs, three monkeys, five cats, five peacocks, two guinea hens, an eagle, a crow, a falcon and an Egyptian crane. Little Allegra whom the Shelleys had brought with them to Italy had been staying with Byron in Ravenna, but he had felt it necessary to send her away from political danger into the safety of a convent.

Revolution was in the air. Though the Italian insurrection against Austria fizzled out, the Greeks had massacred their Turkish masters in the Peloponnese in the spring of 1821. It was not an isolated wave of violence, but part of the popular reaction against autocratic monarchies which followed the Napoleonic wars. Byron was under constant police surveillance. At last in November of that year Byron's close ally, Shelley, cut the knot for him. Shelley arranged for the whole Byron and Gamba households, including of course Teresa, to join him and Mary at Pisa. Byron felt a lingering regret that his new circle was to be English writers and not continental revolutionaries. Italy's '*poetry* of politics' had no doubt become a very limping rhyme. Across the water in Greece, however, the revolution was still rolling. 'I wanted to go to Greece lately,' wrote Byron. But 'the tears of a woman' had again prevailed. In Pisa, however, Byron was introduced by Mary Shelley to the Phanariote Prince Argiropoli, cousin of Prince Mavrocordato, the Greek patriot. It was a link in a new chain.

Teresa and Mary got on well and at first the Pisan circle was harmonious, Byron being established in the splendid Casa Lanfranchi on the Lungarno. But a veritable calendar of unsettling or tragic events occurred in 1822.

In February, Byron's mother-in-law died; his income would expand, thus facilitating activities outside Italy which might tempt him. In March, a serious affray between Byron's servants and a local dragoon made sure that the Pisan, like the Ravenna circle, would eventually be broken up by banishment. In April, Allegra died of fever in her convent, from which Byron had not allowed her to depart, despite the entreaties of Claire and the Shelleys. In May, Byron was invited aboard two visiting American frigates. Entranced by these democrats from the New World, he said he would rather have 'one nod from an American than a snuff-box from an emperor'. His own sailing ship had been christened the *Bolivar*, after the South American liberator. Here were straws in the wind to show which way Byron's heart was moving.

In July, Leigh Hunt arrived, on Shelley's suggestion, to plan with Byron a new magazine, *The Liberal*. Byron's growing restlessness was not assuaged by the presence of the whole Hunt family, whom he had generously settled on his own ground floor – cheerful father, censorious pregnant mother and six undisciplined children. These 'Yahoos', 'little blackguards' or 'Hottentots', as they appeared to him, disfigured the walls of the Casa Lanfranchi with their *graffiti*, much as Byron's menagerie must have decorated the ground floor and staircase of the Palazzo Guiccioli.

Within days of the Hunts' arrival, Shelley was drowned while sailing in his boat the *Don Juan* to Lerici, where he and Mary had taken the Villa Magni (now the Keats-Shelley Museum). In August, the Gambas were exiled from Tuscany and moved to Albarro, near Genoa, hopefully awaiting Byron. In September, Hobhouse arrived at Pisa for a few days and stirred up Byron's interest in the London Committee for aid to Greece, of which Hobby was a member. In October, Byron finally occupied his last Italian residence, the Casa Saluzzo at Albarro.

Though Teresa was actually under the same roof as her lover once more, things could never be the same as in Ravenna. Looked at in one way, Byron's relationship with his *amica* had developed into something deep, tranquil, almost conjugal. In another sense the passion had gone out of it. Byron had to love something passionately. Now it was Greece again – Greece first, last and always.

3 Greece: The Heroic Crusade

The ever-present intention of some day returning to Greece had crystallised quite suddenly in Byron's mind. It could be dated to 5 April 1823. On this day an energetic agent of the London Greek Committee named Edward Blaquiere called on Byron in Genoa, having just received from him a remarkably cordial invitation.

'I have been expecting you for some time,' Byron had written, '– you will find me at home. I cannot express to you how much I feel of interest in the cause, and nothing but the hopes I entertained of witnessing the liberation of Italy itself prevented me long ago from returning to do what little I could, as an individual, in that land which it is an honour even to have visited.' His enthusiasm was genuine. Blaquiere was travelling to Greece on a fact-finding mission from the Committee. What help could the Committee send to the Greek government? At the end of the interview Blaquiere knew that they could send the most glamorous name in Europe – Byron.

Count Pietro Gamba was let into the plot; for plot it would have seemed to poor Teresa if Byron had dared to tell her what was brewing. Pietro's chivalrous imagination caught fire. He was 'devotedly attached to Lord Byron', noted Lady Blessington while on her Italian travels, 'and dreaming of glory and Greece.' Byron was dreaming of Greece and Homer. Don Juan's cynicism was forgotten and Childe Harold's new pilgrimage was conceived in the heroic spirit of Homer rather than of Gothic romance. As proof, Byron was to take with him a wardrobe of brilliant uniforms, an armoury of swords and three helmets, two of them plumed, gilded and Homeric, the third a shako garnished with a figure of the goddess Minerva.

The Homeric helmets have since evoked some ridicule, particularly as Byron was soon to discover how far from heroic were the Committee members in London and the quarrelling factions in Greece. Nevertheless, he was right to boost the Greeks' morale with spectacular displays on ceremonial occasions. Moreover, helmets such as he designed had actually been worn on the field as recently as Waterloo. Both Napoleon's carabiniers and George IV's guards had gone into battle wearing Homeric head-pieces and doubtless deeply impressing one another.

Besides the variety of war-paint, Byron selected (and paid for) a colourful mixture of companions. His young Cornish friend Edward John Trelawny, and his even more youthful Italian doctor Francesco Bruno, did not turn out to be quite all Byron hoped, though without Trelawny's organising ability Byron might never have got to Greece at all, while Bruno's shortcomings were characteristic of his profession at that date.

A word about Trelawny. Gifted and picaresque, 'Tre' or 'T' as his friends called him, seemed the Byronic Corsair come to life. He was darkly handsome, tall and immensely strong. Like the Corsair, he had a mysterious past, in Trelawny's case because he had invented much of it. His *Records of Shelley, Byron and the Author* are sometimes untrustworthy but always irresistible. Byron had met him in Italy with the Shelleys and witnessed the stage-management of Shelley's cremation. 'I knew you were a pagan,' said Byron as he listened to Trelawny's incantations on the beach, 'not that you were a pagan priest.' Or so Trelawney said. Greece was no longer pagan. But it still seemed to Byron companionable and wise to take along a pagan corsair who was dynamic, amusing, good with boats and useful at fighting.

Among his less flamboyant companions were his faithful servants, bluff Captain Scott of the brig *Hercules* which he had hired for the crossing, a young Scottish philhellene named James Hamilton Browne, Pietro Gamba and of course his dogs: the bulldog Moretto and Lyon, a huge Newfoundland. Of his eight servants, the valet Fletcher, the black-bearded ex-gondolier Tita and Lega Zambelli, his accountant, were indispensable. From Trelawny he had bought a negro who called him 'Massa'. Pietro Gamba, possibly fortified by the gift of the 'Minerva' helmet which went to him, while Byron and Trelawny had the Homeric pair – Pietro was given the agonising task of breaking the news of their departure to his sister.

Teresa and Byron each had a presentiment that Greece would be fatal to their love. Byron, indeed, had suffered several changes of heart since the project was first broached. In one mood he would still feel heroic, declaring that there were better things to do for mankind than writing poetry. In another mood he would doubt the capacity of both his health and his purse for the crusade. He had contracted a severe chill after a long swim in the hot sun with Trelawny at Lerici, and his health was still far from robust. Money was a pressing problem. Byron soon found that the London Committee and all sections of the Greek government saw eye to eye on one point at any rate: the rich English lord must be mulcted. Byron was too happy to be of service in this or any other way. He only wondered whether the £10,000 which he had reckoned on could be actually raised by his agent and bankers. (His Newstead estates had been sold five years before.) It was particularly in the company of Lady Blessington that his premonitions surfaced: 'I have a presentiment that I shall die in Greece,' he told her. 'I hope it may be in action, for that would be a good finish to a very *triste* existence, and I have a horror of death-bed scenes.'

The world-weary poet, who was also superstitious, apparently accepted his embarkation date without cavil – 13 July. Two more ill-omened facts followed swiftly. After he had put to sea he twice found himself back again in Genoa harbour, first from a dead calm, then a storm. Were the elements trying to stop him? At this eleventh hour he might have heeded their warning but for one consideration. After his death his banker told Hobhouse that Byron had said *'Hobhouse and the others would laugh at him.'*

4 *Cephalonia : First Days*

It had been a blue and gold September when Byron first approached Greece fourteen years before. The sea was blue and the light golden again. But this time it was parched August and Byron had his special place on deck, swam every day, boxed, fenced and practised his beloved pistol-shooting, the target being poultry hanging from the yard-arm in a basket. As the poultry were to be eaten anyway and Byron was a deadly shot, he may be forgiven for this diversion.

Memories of the earlier Greece crowded in upon him. 'I was happier in Greece,' he said to Trelawny, 'than I have ever been before – or since,' adding that if he had ever written as well as the world said (which he doubted) it was in Greece, or about Greece. When the violet mountains of the Morea at last came up over the horizon, Byron suddenly felt as liberated as Greece herself would soon surely be. 'I don't know why it is,' he reflected, 'but I feel as if the eleven long years of bitterness I have passed through since I was here, were taken off my shoulders and I was scudding through the Greek Archipelago with old Bathurst in his frigate' – the *Salsette*, in which Byron had visited Constantinople and returned to Greece in 1811.

But if Byron's eleven long years had slipped away, Greece's legacy of bitterness was very much with her. The Turkish foe still held certain western fortresses such as Lepanto (Navpaktos), the Castles of Roumeli (Rion) and the Morea (Antirrion), Patras and Corinth, while their fleet controlled the western approaches. Ali Pasha had indeed been murdered in 1822 as we have seen, by his own side, but though this meant one Turkish despot the less, it had been by no means an unqualified blessing for Greece. Ali's liberated domains had split up into several independent regions governed by local primates and *capitani* (civil and military authorities) who felt little loyalty to the national Cause.

What happened here repeated itself on a grander and more tragic scale in Greece as a whole.

By 1823 the spirit of dissension had created two Greeces: Eastern and Western; and two factions, military and constitutional. While the military faction were little better than robber chieftains, the constitutional party were failures. They had lost the bloody battle of Peta, near Arta, against the Turks; and though their esteemed leader, Prince Mavrocordato, had successfully defended Missolonghi during its first siege, he had been voted out of his constitutional position as Chief Executive of the Greek government, and was hiding from his blood-thirsty compatriots on the island of Hydra.

All this and more Byron was soon to hear for himself.

The *Hercules* cast anchor on 3 August 1823, at Argostoli, the capital of Cephalonia and its 60,000 inhabitants situated on the deeply indented, west coast of the island. Cephalonia is the largest of the Ionian Islands which lie off the west coast of Greece. Byron had passed them in 1809, romanticising about Odysseus on Ithaca and Sappho on Levkas. Now he could no longer dream of the past but must think soberly about the neutral British who administered these islands, and whether they might or might not turn a blind eye on his activities for the Cause. As for Odysseus, the modern hero of that name was the clever and ruthless brigand or *klepht* of Eastern Greece, Odysseus Androutses, whose way of life was to prove an irresistible temptation to Trelawny.

Those who know any one of the Ionian Islands will say that it cannot but be the brightest star in the galaxy, so beautiful does it seem: be it Corfu, Levkas, Ithaca, Cephalonia, Zante or another. Those who know them all will nominate them together as the Islands of the Blessed, despite Byron's having already awarded that title to the Cyclades.

The shape of Cephalonia from the air or map is somewhat ungainly, because of its four jutting promontories, the 'back' pair long and the 'front' short. It looks something like a bullfrog diving headlong to the bottom of a pond, followed by a tiny, two-humped fish (Ithaca). But here the uncouthness ends and perfection sets in.

The air of Cephalonia quivers with the brilliant yet soft light which is famous all over Greece, but is marvellously concentrated in this small, mountainous paradise, from every peak of which can be seen the magical Ionian waves. Its sparkling girdle of deep-water coves; its stony paths winding up from the sea through deep green valleys of arbutus, olive, orange and lemon; its handsome mahogany-faced peasants carrying loads of wood and vetch; its rising uplands aromatic with pines, myrtle, lavender and sage; finally, high above Argostoli, its bare indigo and umber plateau of volcanic rock known as the Black Mountain and crowned by the Venetian castle of St George, the capital of the island up till 1757 – all these scenes became familiar and dear to Byron during his five months' stay.

Today nature seems to have changed not at all from Byron's time: the glittering sheen is not smudged nor the stillness broken nor the aromatic perfumes polluted. Nevertheless there has been a vast change made by nature herself in her cruellest mood. The appalling earthquake of 1953 destroyed most of the old houses which Byron would have seen, though the fine long causeway and bridge over the fjord at Argostoli, built by the British in 1813, have survived. At the same time Byron himself was looking at a Cephalonia much changed for the better. This was due to a not inconsiderable human earthquake, the British Governor and Military Resident.

Charles James Napier, a hero of the Peninsular War, had fallen upon Cephalonia in 1822 like a thunderbolt, much as Byron had fallen upon the chambermaid in Calais. He became a father not only to the islanders in general but also of two girls, Susan and Emily, by a Cephaloniot woman

named Anastasia, and persuaded the people to build a dock, a hospital and roads where none had been before. Byron found the going rough everywhere on Cephalonia, but without some of Napier's roads it would have been rougher still.

Napier was away for a few days when the *Hercules* docked at Argostoli. His first exchanges with Byron took place on 5 August on board the *Hercules*, to which Napier was rowed out from the cool and comfortable Residency on the water's edge. 'Lord Byron is here,' he reported home, 'and I like him very much.'

Byron had decided to land at Cephalonia instead of Zante, on Hamilton Browne's advice, precisely because of Napier's known sympathies with the Greek cause. At their first meeting Napier would have described to Byron the unstable situation, illustrating it with a series of thumbnail sketches of the quarrelsome Greek leaders such as he had sent to his brother earlier that year. Odysseus Androutses, Charles had said, was 'one of the ablest Greek chiefs'. 'Colocotronis is a ruffian acquiring riches, but decidedly the chief in the Morea: he is without talent, yet bold and bloody, ridiculing all discipline.' The famous Suliot leader Marco Botsaris had the 'great merit' of being 'a good shot'. (He turned out to have other merits such as self-sacrifice.) Prince Mavrocordato was the 'only gentleman among the chiefs, except for Ypsilanti, who is a goose.' But it was not gentlemanliness alone which made Mavro-cordato stand out. 'Mavrocordato is different,' summed up Napier, 'but dares not offend a chief, for the followers would then quit him, perhaps deliver him to the Turks.' (Six months after Napier wrote this account, the unfortunate Mavrocordato made his escape to Hydra, fearing just such a fate.) Napier had concluded, notwithstanding, with restrained optimism: 'How-ever the cause gets on step by step.' This was to be Byron's own steadfast motto – neither starry-eyed nor discouraged. Napier now invited Byron to stay in the Residency instead of on board ship if he wanted a change.

It was not enough, however, for an ostracised 'Peer of England' (as Byron often signed himself abroad) to be very much liked by the governor of Cephalonia. His mission could still be a failure; he must tread warily. He and his money must not become the cat's paw of either Greek party. His natural indecisiveness found ample justification in the dubious picture of men and events so unexpectedly presented by Napier. Like Napier and the British, Byron must remain neutral, but neutral as between the warring Greek forces instead of between Greeks and Turks. His example, his name, his fame might then draw the two sides together.

Moreover, he must wait for news from the London Committee. Their agent Blaquiere had maddeningly left for England instead of staying, as arranged, to inform Byron of the situation. When would the money from the Committee arrive? Byron's own substantial funds, brought in the form of 30,000 Spanish dollars, an easily convertible currency, must contribute to bringing Mavrocordato back from Hydra and the various Greek squadrons from their bases.

Lastly, Byron needed time to lay up spiritual capital against the great test ahead. The sea voyage had restored his health. But he was still despondent and unsure of himself in this difficult situation. It needed time for Napier's magic to work.

The only partisan exception he would make was for his beloved Suliots. Here they were again, in Cephalonia, complete with capotes and war-songs. They had suffered yet another exodus from their Suli strongholds in 1822 and been settled by the resourceful Napier. Not that Byron's companions shared his enthusiasm for these rapacious chieftains. When a crowd of Suliots invaded the *Hercules* on her arrival, Trelawny described the scene in terms of zoo life: the 'Zuliotes' he saw as vultures and jackals, Lega Zambelli as a viper 'coiled on the money-chest' and Byron 'at bay like a hunted lion'. Captain Scott referred to them contemptuously as 'Zodiacs'.

Byron's loyalty to the rough comrades of his youth remained unshakable. He recruited what Trelawny would have called a 'pack' of Suliots and paid all their expenses out of his own pocket.

Meanwhile life on board the *Hercules* anchored in that warm sea was far from drear. Every day Byron and Trelawny would swim from a rock across the harbour, afterwards supping under the olive trees on shore. There was much social life, for Byron was nothing if not sparkling in company. He and Napier shared a common taste in laughter and mockery. Strangely, Byron also shared a common taste for religious discussion with a proselitising Methodist doctor named James Kennedy, who attended the garrison. Argostoli was alive with good causes that summer. This pleasant waiting period was the ideal time for a short expedition. Byron decided to visit Ithaca, another 'greenest island' of his imagination, on 11 August.

5 Ithaca : The Beatific Vision

A hard first day lay ahead for Byron's party consisting of himself, Pietro Gamba, Trelawny, Hamilton Browne, Dr Bruno and the servants. Setting out at dawn in a cavalcade of mules across the long bridge of Argostoli, it took them nine burning hours to reach Cephalonia's St Euphemia, the nearest port to the small landing-place on Ithaca. The central massif of Cephalonia bisects the island sometimes rising to a height of over 5000 feet, and it was across these tumbled rocks and forests that Byron had to pass under the sun of midday.

From St Euphemia they could see the little white houses of Sami shimmering at the southern end of Samis Bay. Within a week 'poor B', as he used to

call himself whimsically in youth, would be suffering horrible physical and
mental paroxysms among the dark pines above those houses. But for the
moment the voyage across the Ithaca strait in an open boat was pure joy to
him. Again, as on his arrival in the Ionian Sea a week or so earlier, he felt the
'long years of bitterness' were slipping from him and he was once more
young.

The port for Ithaca today, when setting out from Argostoli, is not St
Euphemia but Sami. The car swoops up and down between the pines of a
metal road till it reaches the small square and quay of Sami in an hour or so.
Byron was rowed across in a four-oared open boat and it took him all the
afternoon until sunset to reach Ithaca; a caïque driven by oil, like the little
Maria, makes the trip in one hour. But it will have been the same halcyon day
for each. Where the deep blue water ripples beside the boat, the shadows are
truly 'wine-dark' as Homer said – a red-purple wine, not the inky-blue home-
made brew one is generously offered at the monastery perched on a dizzy
Ithacan peak. As the mainland of Cephalonia recedes, its mountain ranges
subside into gentle curves, with mist layered between the different shades of
blue, so that only their outlines stand out sharp and clear. The lonely cove

and harbour on Ithaca soon become faintly visible. At a distance its mountains look bare. A white road zig-zags up from the bay between the limestone hills until it disappears across the isthmus to Vathy, Ithaca's capital.

When Byron's party arrived at sunset the place was empty. No mules, no men to meet him and guide him inland. Today, visitors, if they have remembered to make a telephone call in advance, are luckier. As their boat glides gently towards the exquisite, deserted cove they can watch a pair of small black beetles crawling one behind the other down the white road, which turn out to be taxis.

Byron was perfectly happy in his predicament. Knowledge of Homer and personal observation told him that the coast was perforated with caves. He could see them, dark holes in the creamy limestone, as the boat approached the shore. In gathering dusk he decided to settle for one of those salty caverns as his home for the night.

From the top of the hill, however, above the harbour, Pietro and Hamilton Browne did some reconnoitring and eventually came upon the house of a refugee merchant from Trieste, who put them all up in one small room. They were determined that their friend and leader should not run the risk of that nineteenth-century killer, the 'night air'.

Next morning Byron made sure he got a little of the cave life he loved. While his friends were contacting Captain Knox, the British Resident at Vathy, and coming back in a boat to fetch him, the poet discovered another cavern, known as 'Ulysses' (or Odysseus') stronghold', and was found fast asleep at the entrance enjoying a 'beatific dream or vision'. He was annoyed to be woken from his dream in order to have an inferior vision of the Residency at Vathy.

Nevertheless, Vathy was a small dream town of white houses, strung along the deep end of a horseshoe formed by the vine-terraced hills around the bay. (Vathy or 'Bathus' means deep.) The depth of the inlet on which Vathy stands so prettily is matched by the deep waters beneath – modern liners can anchor here – not forgetting their unbelievably deep colour. All this beauty in its Homeric setting made Byron peculiarly expansive that evening in the Residency, where he met a certain Thomas Smith. As if he had known Smith for years, he talked of things near his heart like the Greek cause, his poetry, his wife, his daughter Ada. Apropos of Greeks he made a remark which should comfort all disillusioned do-gooders: 'We must not always look too closely at the men who are to benefit by our exertions in a good cause, as God knows we shall seldom do much good in this world.'

An expedition to the 'Fountain of Arethusa' took place on the following day. It was a five-mile ride from Vathy along a mule track to one of Ithaca's green valleys, and then up a cliff path to the (modern) springs of Perapigadi. Here had stood the legendary hut of Eumaeus, the swineherd in Homer's *Odyssey*, in which he sheltered the returning Odysseus disguised as a beggar.

Eumaeus had also been lucky enough to surprise the goddess Arethusa bathing, while bringing his swine for a drink. Byron's party surprised nothing more than two goatherds in a cavern, who piped Albanian tunes which Browne ungratefully found 'discordant'.

These Albanian goatherds were two of the many refugees from the mainland who landed up in Ithaca instead of Cephalonia. Byron was to help them all with a generous expenditure of money – 250 dollars left with the governor. One family in particular, that of Chalandritsanos from the Morea, he was to support individually, having brought them from Ithaca to Cephalonia with unforeseeable consequences to his own peace of mind.

Byron's last excursion on Ithaca was by boat to the hills north of the isthmus, where one of the many Mycenaean outcrops on the island was known as the 'School of Homer'. A nineteenth-century print of the 'School' shows indeterminate classical ruins with figures. Byron was at his gayest, joking with Mrs 'Penelope' and Master 'Telemachus' Knox, as he called his hostess and her son, and summoning Tita to bring tumblers of gin-and-water all round – the true Pierian spring and source of all poetry, in Byron's mocking words. He dined contentedly on cold fish and green salad with the orthodox Greeks present, since it was a Greek fast, instead of on the roast beef provided for the British.

This abstemiousness, as well as being characteristic of Byron in certain moods, may also have been a subtle dig at an old acquaintance, the 'free-thinking' bishop whom 'Childe Harold' had met at Livadia, as we saw, during his first pilgrimage. On that occasion the Childe had brusquely decided that the bishop's unorthodox ideas did him little credit. Now, when the bishop reappeared unexpectedly, Byron accepted his warm salutation of a kiss for old time's sake, despite the bristly beard on his chin and the garlic on his breath.

As they returned from the School of Homer a storm blew up, to Byron's delight. 'I don't know if you all swim, gentlemen,' he said to his friends; 'but if you do you will have fifty fathoms of blue water to support you; and if you do not, you will have it over you.' After further teasing of the expert sailor, Trelawny, by giving him nautical advice ('Starboard, Trelawny – bring her up. There! she is trim') Byron ordered another swig all round at the Pierian spring. *'Tita, i fiaschi!'*

On the fifth and last morning in Ithaca, 16 August, the party began their return to Cephalonia. Mounted on ponies they rode to the verdant saddle between Ithaca's two mountains, and then up and down over the delightfully resinous hills between tall firs, clumps of broom, gorse and herbs, and small or large-leaved cistus, which in spring would be spattered with gold, white, rose and purple but which now in August poured their pungent scent over the blinding white track.

They reached the jetty well before the boat from St Euphemia. As one

A view from Olympia.

OVERLEAF, LEFT Across the bay in Cephalonia from Sami monastery. RIGHT The island of Ithaca with the town of Vathy at the end of the horseshoe bay.

would expect, Byron, with his passion for the 'fathoms of blue water' and after such a long hot ride, sprang into the warm sea and 'exhibited various feats in swimming'. These 'feats' may have been racing Trelawny or diving for shells and pebbles on the seabed – all pretty strenuous. The water in that remote harbour is as inviting today as it was then. Shoals of tiny fish dart to and fro and nothing more polluting is seen than a few fish skeletons of a deathly pale green far below.

It was while waiting for the boat, and perhaps beginning to feel unwell from the blazing sun on his wet curls, that Byron delivered one of his most caustic denunciations of literary sight-seeing. How much he must have enjoyed the 'classical remembrances' of Homer's island, volunteered Browne. 'You quite mistake me,' retorted Byron; 'I have no poetical humbug about me. I am too old for that. Ideas of that sort are confined to rhyme.'

Trelawny gives a vivid account of what must have been the same conversation. Characteristically, however, he misplaces it, dating it to the first day of the expedition instead of the last. When it was proposed, says Trelawny, that Byron should visit 'some of the localities that antiquaries have dubbed with the title of Homer's school, – Ulysses' stronghold, &c . . .' he burst into a petulant protest. 'Do I look like one of those emasculated fogeys? Let's have a swim. I detest antiquarian twaddle.' According to Trelawny, Byron then expressed sentiments about 'rhyme' which fit remarkably well with the account given by Browne. 'Do people think I have no lucid intervals, that I came to Greece to scribble more nonsense? I will show I can do something better: I wish I had never written a line, for having it cast in my teeth at every turn.'

One particularly attractive description of Ithaca by Trelawny may represent his memory of the Fountain of Arethusa telescoped with the party's final return to the cove: 'The next day we retraced our steps through the flowery ravines and tranquil glades of this lovely islet, our road winding along the foot of the mountains. The grey olive-trees, bright green fig, and rampant vine, that grew above our heads, screened us from the sun; the fresh breeze from the sea, with the springs of purest water gushing out of the rocks, soothed the Poet's temper. He turned out of the path to look at a natural grotto, in a grove of forest trees, and said "You will find nothing in Greece or its islands so pleasant as this. If this isle were mine – I would break my staff and bury my book. . . ."'

We must be grateful to Trelawny for this memory. Byron's second pilgrimage to Greece did indeed make him something of a Prospero, breaking the magic staff of his poetry and burying the book in which *Don Juan* still lay unfinished. The 'love of women' was buried in the same grave: *Our revels now are ended. . . . We'll go no more a-roving. . . .*

But Byron was a Prospero with a difference. On ceasing to 'rhyme' and dream, he would act.

A solitary stake in the sea at Missolonghi.

6 Sami : The Nightmare

As they approached Cephalonia again over the brilliant sea, a white tower and walls would gradually have become visible among the dark pines above Sami. This was the monastery of St Cosmas on Mt Agrilion, scene of the contretemps already mentioned.

They disembarked at St Euphemia early in the afternoon, still under a blazing sky. A formidable dinner of rich foods and wine had been prepared in Byron's honour. It was the worst thing for him, but he had neither the strength of mind nor the incivility to refuse. After many festive hours the party rode off in the falling dusk to spend the night at the white monastery on the far headland of Sami.

There had been signs on Ithaca that Byron's health had not fully recovered from his illness at Lerici. Thomas Smith had noticed him coming up the beach at Vathy on 14 August looking 'like a man under sentence of death' – pale, shrunk, languid, ghastly. That same night, Dr Bruno afterwards told Browne, he had been gravely ill and 'saved' only by 'blessed pills' *(benedette pillule)*. These gloomy portents were to be fulfilled during the night of the 16th.

Though not many hundred feet above sea level, the monastery at Sami was reached by a steep climb. The first thing Byron noticed at the top were some open sarcophagi standing under the white walls, no doubt to receive the next monks in their coffins. Instead, one of them received Lord Byron, who clambered into the deepest, lay full length at the bottom and began reciting 'Alas, poor Yorick', from *Hamlet*. Of course this behaviour in itself did not mean that Byron's mind was seriously disturbed. After all, he had long ago developed his 'grave fixation', dreaming in Harrow churchyard, collecting the Newstead and Athenian skulls, and composing a poem on Charles Churchill's grave above Dover. Moreover, to lie down in a coffin, your own or someone else's, was not unheard of even as late as the nineteenth-century, though it might be taken to mean that the performer had a premonition of death. Sir Thomas Picton had done it in Wales shortly before going to the front and dying at Waterloo.

Byron's restful pastime was interrupted by the sight of a torch-light procession, grey-gowned monks chanting and swinging censers and a 'whining dotard' (the abbot) leading the preliminary ceremonies of the evening in the 'Lordo Inglese's' honour. The exhausted poet lost patience. Having acted Hamlet in the sarcophagus, he suddenly switched to the part of Henry II. When the abbot reached his *pièce de resistance*, an interminable and flowery address delivered in the usual nasal tones of Greek orthodoxy, Byron shouted, 'Will no one relieve me from the presence of this pestilential mad-man?'

But who was the madman? The abbot, dolefully touching his own

A monk outside the small chamber which is believed to have been Byron's guest room.

forehead, said in a tremulous voice, 'Poor fellow, he is mad.' For Byron, with burning brow, flashing eyes and violent spasms in his stomach and liver, had snatched up a lamp and 'darted' into the nearest bedroom where he tore to shreds half his own clothes and all the bedding, smashed up articles of furniture, barricaded himself into a corner and faced his persecutors like a lion at bay. Young Dr Bruno must have been too terrified to approach him even with the 'blessed pills'. Trelawny and Smith bravely tried and failed. 'Baih! out, out of my sight!' screamed the Pilgrim; 'Fiends, can I have no peace, no relief from this hell! Leave me, I say', hurling a chair at Smith's head. At last Hamilton Browne calmed him down, got two *benedette pillule* down his throat, and a stunned silence reigned over St Cosmas for the rest of that night.

'Poor B' was overwhelmed with remorse next day, and paid marked respect to the abbot. Starting at midday the party rode from Sami back to Argostoli and the *Hercules*. The road may have been one of those improved by Napier, for it was smoother and wider than that to St Euphemia. There were no mishaps. Byron sang a selection of Tom Moore's melodies and popular street songs in a cockney accent as he jogged along. On either side stood olive groves and ranks of tall cypresses, said to be planted as dowries for the islanders' daughters. Above, the limestone lay exposed on the mountain sides like white bones.

It is a curious fact that Trelawny places the monastery in which Byron had his seizure on Ithaca not Cephalonia. Curious, because there is indeed a monastery on Ithaca which fits Trelawny's description exactly, much better than Sami.

The Virgin's chapel and monastic buildings on Ithaca's Mt Katharon hang dizzily above the sea. The ascent is long, precipitous and arduous, just as Trelawny says, and quite unlike the moderate climb to Sami. So high is Mt Katharon that one feels the white building on the summit will turn out to be a light-house. Trelawny writes of 'the magnificent view of the Ionian Sea, Greece, and many islands'. True enough of Mt Katharon but not of Mt Agrilion, which faces east towards the mainland and is not exceptionally lofty. Moreover the Sami monastery is not on its summit.

Trelawny, publishing first in 1858, dates the excursion to this monastery to the second day on Ithaca, 12 August; whereas according to Browne's account, the whole of their second day was occupied with retrieving Byron from under the wild fig-tree and getting to Vathy. Trelawny remembers Byron having had a long swim immediately after arriving on Ithaca (which at least sounds likely) followed by a scramble up the rocks on the shore, and a sleep and 'dream' outside the cave. After which the party spent the night in a goat-herd's cottage. According to Trelawny, they rode next morning the six miles to Vathy and struggled to the top of towering Mt Katharon, to visit its monastery, that same afternoon. A prodigiously

The interior of Byron's room at Sami.

ΛΟΡΔΟΣ ΒΥΡΩΝ

"Τῶν ἀνδρῶν τῶν
ὑπερόχων εἶναι τάφος ἡ γῆ...

exhausting day; enough to give every one of them seizures – except of course the superman 'Tre'.

Were Browne and Smith wrong and Trelawny right as between Ithaca and Cephalonia for the location of Byron's 'Nightmare Monastery'? After some hesitation because of the striking likeness between the Mt Katharon of Ithaca and Trelawny's description, I have come to feel with Byron's principal biographers that 'Tre' was wrong. His chronology is unacceptable. There is no tradition on Ithaca of Byron's visiting this monastery, whereas, as we shall see, the tradition at Sami is strong. Above all, Trelawny always exaggerated. Everything he saw and did was the biggest. The cap fits Ithaca rather than Sami simply because the former monastery is much higher, and Trelawny could not describe anything except in outsize terms.

Trelawny's account of the monastery episode was rounded off by yet another macabre story of 'poor B'. If one accepts Trelawny's capricious time-table, Byron got back into his cabin on the *Hercules* at 2 a.m. after crossing the sea on the last day. Roused by Trelawny some ten hours later, he started up in terror, stared wildly at his friend and said with a convulsive sigh, 'I have had such a dream! I am trembling with fear. I am not fit to go to Greece.... If you had come to strangle me I could have done nothing.' 'Who could against a nightmare?' replied Trelawny. Then, pointing to the brace of silver-mounted pistols and the bible Augusta had given Byron, both of which prophylactics he always kept by his bedside, Trelawny said, 'The hag don't mind your pistols or your bible.'

Today at the monastery above Sami there is no thought of madness, hag, nightmare or pistols in connection with Byron. The monks remembered Byron on 28 April 1974, a date as near as possible to the 150th anniversary of his death, with moving ceremonies. Inside the chapel a small 'shrine' had been erected on which stood a bold pen-portrait of the poet sketched by a Greek schoolboy, with an adapted extract in modern Greek from Pericles' famous funeral oration: 'All the earth is the tomb of famous men.' Below lay a laurel wreath bound with ribbons of Greek blue.

The memorial service inside the chapel was conducted by the monks and attended by dignitaries from the towns of Sami and friends of Byron from far afield. As the eulogies were delivered and the required nasal responses sung from behind the screen, Byron's ghost may have smiled. Candles were lit to St Cosmas and the rood-screen admired. But cracks could be detected in the paint and gilding, reminding us of the devastating earthquake which had torn Cephalonia to pieces twenty-one years before.

Outside, few of the old monastery buildings remain. One narrow white-washed room, however, with eight short rafters eighteen inches apart across the low ceiling, is shown as the guest chamber where Byron stayed. A coloured mid-nineteenth-century portrait of the poet presides over the now peaceful scene.

A Greek schoolboy stands inside the chapel at Sami with his sketch of Byron.

143

The monastery tower still stands, but so shaken that it is not safe to climb and is no longer used. Its three bells hang below the branches of a gnarled olive tree beside it, like three thieves; but time, which has filched so much, has not stolen the memory of Byron.

The three monastery bells survive since Byron's time.

7 Metaxata : 'Cool Serenity'

A week away from his HQ at Cephalonia brought no news from the English Committee or Greek Government, and consequently no changes in Byron's policy of waiting. If anything, the argument for delay was strengthened by events during the second half of August.

There were signs that Greek dissensions were increasing rather than dwindling. The longer Byron spent on Cephalonia the better his presence became known, and the more he was badgered by Greeks of all factions with demands for his dollars to use against the Turks, or more likely, one another. In Canto X of *Don Juan*, Byron had reprimanded the renowned prison reformer, Mrs Elizabeth Fry, for preaching to the '*poor* rogues' of Newgate, instead of to their betters. Now, from the Ionian Islands, he admitted that there was room for a Mrs Fry – on the Greek mainland. But not to lambaste a people who had been corrupted by many centuries of slavery. 'Whoever goes into Greece at present,' he wrote in his journal, 'should do it as Mrs Fry went into Newgate . . . in the hope that time and better treatment will reclaim the present burglarious and larcenous tendencies which have followed this General Gaol delivery. . . .'

His beloved Suliots seemed to have become a rather prominent feature of the 'General Gaol delivery'. Their wildness and unbridled greed finally persuaded him to return a large number of them into their own mountains, complete with a month's pay and their weapons. But he would not denounce them in public. 'Of the Greeks I shall say nothing,' he wrote to his banker, 'till I can say something better, except that I am not discouraged. . . .'

Momentarily, there had been a sign on 18 August that Byron's weeks of waiting might soon be brought to an end. A glowing invitation was despatched to him by that 'very good shot' and best of Suliot leaders, Marco Botsaris. This dedicated warrior was holding off a Turkish attack above Missolonghi. With a force of only 350 Suliots, he felt that the addition of Byron's own Suliots would make all the difference. 'Let nothing prevent you from coming into this part of Greece,' he wrote; '. . . The day after tomorrow I will set out, with a few chosen companions, to meet your Excellency. Do not delay.'

But 'the day after tomorrow' was to be the eve of Marco's last fight. He was shot through the head on 21 August, the day before Byron received his invitation. If Botsaris had lived, Byron might have gone to Missolonghi four months earlier than he did, perhaps also to die like the noble Suliot from a bullet, instead of from bleeding and the bark.

Descendants of Marco Botsaris still live in Athens. His piercing eyes still stare out from many picture-frames above his splendid mustachios and beneath a red cap with gold tassel. The present General Botsaris possesses the white silk banner which Marco carried into battle at his death. It had been presented to a member of his family by Catherine the Great, who fancied him much as she fancied 'Don Juan' in Byron's poem. On one side of the banner St George slays the dragon, on the other St Demetrius prods a monster. There are scattered brown bloodstains on the silk, and signs that it was torn from the pole when Marco fell, the better to bring it away safely. Among the pictures and emblems on the General's walls are also Suliot pistols, swords and knives. A giant musket takes pride of place. Five or six feet long, it is so heavy that two Suliot soldiers were needed to bring it into action: one held it on his shoulder while the other fired.

Marco Botsaris and (left) the white silk banner which he carried into battle.

RIGHT A long Suliot musket operated by two soldiers.

These troubles did not prevent Byron from enjoying the second half of his stay on board the *Hercules* at Argostoli. His health was again improving, through a meagre diet of tea, vegetables and cheese. This could be relaxed at discretion. One such occasion occurred when, to Byron's agreeable surprise, the officers of the garrison invited the 'wicked lord' to dinner. He accepted, was toasted, and replied in a nervous speech which betrayed his anxiety to please. He might well be somewhat apprehensive, knowing how much tact was needed in this enclave of British neutrality. Yet there he stood in his refulgent uniform (fortunately more Ruritanian than Greek), preparing at any moment now to enter the war. His charm and wit swept away all embarrassment. The officers praised his *Corsair* and perhaps hinted, with a flattering glance at his *Hebrew Melodies*, that if Byron chose to descend like a wolf on the Turkish fold, who were they to criticise him?

That other Corsair, Trelawny, seems to have suddenly got restive when Byron and his party left the *Hercules* on 2 September and went ashore. 'I well knew that once on shore,' he wrote in 1858, 'Byron would fall back on his old routine of dawdling habits, plotting – planning – shilly-shallying – and doing nothing. It was a maxim of his, "If I am stopped for six days at any place, I cannot be made to move for six months."'

It was a pity Byron did not spend six months on shore in Cephalonia instead of only four. He would then have missed much of the rainy season in Missolonghi and perhaps lived. Trelawny and Browne, meanwhile, did not accompany Byron to his new inland house. Byron sent them with letters to the Greek government at Tripolitza, in one more effort to find out how he could best serve.

'Let me hear from you often,' he said in parting from Trelawny, '– come back soon.' Trelawny never came back. He went a-roving with the robber-chief Odysseus Androutses in Eastern Greece, where the latter was conduct-ing his own war against the Turks. Byron's last words to him showed that the 'dawdling' poet had a shrewd idea of the state of things on the mainland. After having told Trelawny to keep him posted with news, he added, 'If things are farcical they will do for "Don Juan"; if heroical, you have another canto of "Childe Harold".'

It was to be 'Don Juan' all the way, though not just because of the Greeks. Nor, alas, were the farcical things to be immortalised in that great poem. Prospero's book remained buried. But at least there were to be many more halcyon weeks in Cephalonia before the farce drifted into tragedy.

Metaxata was the name of Byron's inland retreat on Cephalonia. Standing at the window of his villa he wrote of 'this beautiful village' from which he could see in the 'calm though cool serenity' of 'transparent moonlight', the Islands, mountains, sea, 'with a distant outline of the Morea between the double azure of the waves and skies. . . .'

Most of 'this beautiful village' has been destroyed by the earthquake of 1953, including Byron's house. But the airy situation, the groups of palm trees, the graceful cypresses, the narrow alleys and the green gardens behind the high stone walls are as attractive as ever. From the gate of one of these gardens can be seen a monumental clump of ivy. It is known as 'Byron's Ivy', and legend has it that he planted the first shoots.

The village lies a few miles from Argostoli in the centre of low fertile hills which rise in a semicircle from the Ionian Sea. Where there are rocks, a frilly edging of white foam finishes off the arc of green fields. A long smooth strip of grass has recently slashed like a sword across these fields close by the sea, a runway. But when Byron looked down from the window or balcony of his small, charming villa he saw only the dark gloss of orange and lemon trees, the yellowing vines, grey olives and blue water dotted with green or misty isles, between himself and the beckoning mainland.

He had no wish to answer that summons until he had received all his 'advices' and weighed up the multiplying requests. Count Metaxa wanted him at Missolonghi, Prince Mavrocordato wanted him at Hydra, the London Committee wanted him as their representative with the Greek government to take delivery of stores on their way from England. He wrote letters to everybody, even sometimes to Teresa, though usually he sent her only a postscript in one of Pietro's letters. What a life for a poet. Or as Byron quoted to Augusta, '"Oh! Plato, what a task for a Philosopher!"'

Just outside Lakythra, the next village to Metaxata, a stony lane is shadowed by trees. It leads to a little white chapel on a hill, and a group of flat grey rocks lying on the green turf, with a glorious view of the sea.

Metaxata is just visible among its groves. On these rocks Byron would sit writing. The villagers thought that he must be writing poetry, and so he would have been but for the Cause. Instead, it was his journal or the interminable letters – a bore for him but superb entertainment for us. To Napier he would describe his efforts to unite the Greek factions as 'bear-taming'. To Augusta he would nominate Mavrocordato as the only 'Washington' kind of man among them. To Teresa he would write tactfully, 'I was a fool to come here; but, being here, I must see what is to be done.'

148

Nevertheless, the tradition of his poetry-writing at Lakythra lives on. A glittering white marble slab lies upon the largest rock bearing a memorable inscription in Greek capitals: IF I AM A POET I OWE IT TO THE AIR OF GREECE. BYRON.

Down in the village a signpost points up the hill with the appealing direction, 'Byron Roci'.

Pietro Gamba, who was among those staying with Byron at Metaxata, received in conversation a more penetrating impression of the poet's feeling for Greece. 'If Greece should fall,' he burst out, 'I will bury myself in the ruins!' Meanwhile, his 'hermit's life' (Pietro's phrase) was pleasantly varied by visits from the British officers at Argostoli and local festivities. James

Priests outside the church
at Lakythra where Byron
would sit on the flat
rocks writing.

Kennedy, the garrison's Methodist doctor, renewed his efforts to convert 'Cain'. The resources of Metaxata included daily rides for Byron and his friends 'and sometimes we are given', wrote Pietro to Teresa, 'a fine dance, which is not too agreeable.' Whatever Pietro may have thought of local gaieties (if this is what he meant), anyone who has had the good fortune to watch Cephaloniot dances will think them not only highly agreeable but moving and revealing of the islanders' story. Byron has described the Greek dancing on Haidée's island in *Don Juan*, drawing on the experiences of his first pilgrimage:

> *And further on a troop of Grecian girls,*
> > *The first and tallest her white kerchief waving,*
> *Were strung together like a row of pearls,*
> > *Linked hand in hand, and dancing. . . .*

On Cephalonia also the girls are 'strung together like a row of pearls', but wearing their distinctive national dress: a large white kerchief or head-scarf with one end flung over the left shoulder and the other hanging to the waist, scarlet bodice faced with yellow, full white sleeves, long dark-blue skirt and pale-blue apron with yellow diagonal stripes. Their history of successive occupations by foreigners as well as the various influxes of Suliot refugees with their own dramatic traditions, give the dances a special focus. The defiance of the Suliot women by sacrificing themselves and their children is acted out in the dance. A choral song accompanied by a mandolin has the melancholy overtones of the Volga Boatman.

But it is by the men's dances that the national spirit is most vividly conveyed. 'Linked hand in hand', or rather by a coloured handkerchief in each hand, the men bound to and fro, while more bright handkerchiefs suspended around their white kilts add a swirling motion to the windings of the chain. This unbroken but flexible chain suggests a people sticking together and supporting one another.

Early in October the 'cool serenity' of Metaxata was rudely shaken by a series of earthquake shocks. The disproportion between the damage and the panic greatly amused the 'Don Juan' in Byron, who regaled Augusta with an account of wild leapings from windows and landings. He himself walked down the stairs and out of the door.

The chief break, however, in weeks of 'cool serenity' was caused by the arrival in Greece of yet another of the eccentric Stanhopes – this time, Colonel the Honourable Leicester Stanhope, eldest son of Lord Harrington. A leading member of the London Committee and now appointed their agent in Greece, Stanhope typified the doctrinaire theoreticians who conducted its affairs. Many of them were more concerned with the spread of Utilitarianism than with the Greek War of Independence. Their faith in education, literacy and a free press in Greece was of course a long-term winner; but in the short term these admirable principles would not beat the Turks. When Stanhope recorded that his mightiest weapon was to be a printing-press, to print news-papers for a Greece which could scarcely read, Byron nicknamed him wryly 'the typographical Colonel'. But notwithstanding these eccentricities, Colonel Stanhope at any rate was a real soldier and what Napier called 'a doing man'. His energy was needed since Byron's mainstay, Colonel Napier himself, was about to leave for home.

Napier hoped, on Byron's recommendation, to organise and bring out a regular force from England. In the event both the British government and the Greek Committee were to let him and Byron down. The government made it plain that Napier would lose his commission in the British army if he fought for Greece. The Committee, whom in any case Napier regarded as 'a set of ninicoms', could not guarantee his pay. They could afford to send out to Greece 'water-colours, trumpets, fine drapes, to fight the Turks' – but not Napier. Thus Byron lost his best soldier and most congenial counsellor.

He too, like Napier, regarded the trumpets, in particular, with despair – unless, of course, those vast walls of Constantinople which he had admired so much in 1810 were to fall flat at the sound of a trumpet like the walls of Jericho.

The eagles were gathering at Missolonghi, if not yet the vultures. How much longer could Byron resist the mounting pressures to join them? The situation was still obscure, even dangerously like a civil war. But Trelawny had called him irresolute; Stanhope said he lacked push – before pushing off himself to Missolonghi and leaving Byron to bring over the printing-press. Greek deputies had gone to England to arrange for the raising of a substantial loan by the Committee, and Byron was to be its Commissioner. He had launched the Hydriot squadron by advancing £4000 of his own money. He had sold all his Italian possessions except his treasured 'Napoleonic' carriage, in which he had travelled to Italy. He heard that 'all the world' were awaiting him at Missolonghi 'with feverish anxiety', primates, *capitani*, Suliots. The whole Suliot body had chosen him to be their personal chief – and paymaster. Prince Mavrocordato was there, promising that Byron's counsels would be listened to 'like oracles'. Stanhope told him that while walking along the street on 28 December he had been stopped by people asking after Lord Byron!!! (Stanhope added the three exclamation marks as a matter of urgency.)

By 26 December Byron had left Metaxata, his 'beautiful village', for ever. He spent two more days in Argostoli. He still thought that 'none of the Greeks know a problem from a poker' – but 'in for a penny in for a pound' – plenty of pounds. He would never stop repeating what he had said to his banker in October – 'As I have embarked in the Cause, I won't quit it. . . .' The Cause demanded that he should embark in a Cephaloniot mistico, a long light fast craft, on 28 December, *en route* for Missolonghi.

8   The Ionian Sea : Misadventures

The voyage did not lack adventure. But first Byron must call at the island of Zante, a rounded green hump like a cabochon emerald, which he had been able to see from the enchanted windows at Metaxata. After being weatherbound in port at Argostoli for two days, they reached Zante early on the morning of the 30th. Stanhope reported to London that the 'Messiah', as the people saw Byron, was coming.

Zante, the most flowery of all the Ionian Islands, abounds in gardens and overflows with the riches of currant vineyards and olive groves. Here was born Solomos in 1798, ten years after Byron, the great Greek national poet, who was later to celebrate Byron in his songs. Greek scholars are today convinced that Solomos went on board Byron's mistico at Zante to greet him.

There was an old Venetian castle above Zakinthos, the capital of Zante and now the name of the whole island. From the castle hill, Byron could have seen as far as the featureless promontory of Missolonghi sticking out to sea on his left, and Navarino Bay on his right; the one where he was to die, the other where the whole Turkish fleet was to be destroyed. But this was no time to go a-roving or a-riding up to the tops of hills by the light of the moon, as in the summer and autumn days on Ithaca and Cephalonia. It was wet mid-winter. The rains would splash and drip for a whole season ahead. The sands were running out.

Byron did not even land on Zante though the Resident was 'as kind as could be', came on board and offered him every hospitality. He did not need hospitality, however, but cash. His agent at Zante, Samuel Barff, the noted philhellene banker and merchant, brought him 8000 dollars; 'But I foresee,' wrote Byron, 'that we shall have occasion for all the cash I can muster at Zante and elsewhere. . . .'

The mistico, accompanied by her consort, a bombard, both sailed that evening. Byron had filled the big bombard with baggage, servants, and all the Committee's 'stuff', as he called it, including Stanhope's printing-press; the whole in charge of Pietro Gamba and the bull-dog Moretto. The mistico was to race ahead carrying Byron, his handsome page Lukas Chalandritsanos, the Newfoundland dog Lyon, Dr Bruno, Tita and Fletcher.

Pietro has left a debonair picture of the departure. For the first four hours bombard and mistico sailed together, driven onwards by patriotic songs and a smart breeze. Then the mistico began to draw away from the bombard, though salvoes of pistols and carbines kept them in touch for two more hours. By midnight they were set on their separate, adventurous courses. Pietro still thought it was to be 'Missolonghi–tomorrow'. But tomorrow, *avrion*, is a long time in Greek. In fact, neither of them was to arrive 'tomorrow'.

As luck – and Greek negligence – would have it, Turkish frigates had slipped from Patras and were patrolling the deep waters in front of Misso-longhi, unknown to the bombard and mistico. 'But where the devil is the fleet gone? – the Greek, I mean,' Byron was to write angrily to Stanhope; 'leaving us to get in without the least intimation to take heed that the Moslems were out again.' The unfortunate bombard was hailed at dawn by an enemy frigate, and but for the coincidence that her captain had once saved his Turkish opposite number from shipwreck in the Black Sea, would have been sent to the bottom. As it was, Gamba surreptitiously sent Byron's correspond-ence to the bottom for fear of its falling into enemy hands, before he and all of them were handed over to the Pasha at Patras. However, the good offices of the Turkish captain secured their release. Byron afterwards liked to follow the Greeks in calling it a miracle. 'I attribute their release entirely to Saint Dionysius, of Zante, and the Madonna of the Rock, near Cephalonia.' The bombard arrived in Missolonghi on 4 January – to find no Byron.

Byron, meanwhile, had escaped a Turkish force earlier on the morning of 31 December at 2 a.m., after a near miss and instant evasive action. At dawn they could see one frigate chasing the bombard and another blocking Missolonghi. They dashed for the shelter of the Scrofes rocks. Byron was desperately alarmed for the boy Lukas. 'I would sooner cut him in pieces, and myself too, than have him taken out by those barbarians.' Even the level-headed Napier had once spoken of the Turks chopping the Greeks into kebabs. Similar concern had been felt by Byron for young Robert Rushton in 1809, though with a good deal less cause.

Now the mistico managed to land Lukas near Anatolico, where the youthful Byron and Hobhouse had once spent the night. Hardly had Lukas begun his trek overland to Missolonghi before the Turkish frigate guarding the port hove in sight. Away sped the mistico again from creek to creek, first westward along the rocky coast, and then due north, past where the River Achelous poured into the sea, until they reached a safe haven at Drago-mestre (modern Astakos).

The river-god Achelous had been born of the Titans, Oceanus and Thetys. Byron knew from of old the hazards of this savage Akarnanian country through which the Achelous flowed, and which indeed seemed to belong to some earlier, more savage creation. He wisely declined to go ashore, though civilly invited by the primates of Dragomestre. He stayed on board guarding his dollars, if not like a viper, like Lega Zambelli on first arriving at Argostoli. New Year's Day, 1824, was spent at Dragomestre writing an account of his plight to Prince Mavrocordato and awaiting rescue. Next day an escort of three gun-boats arrived from Missolonghi, the Prince advising against a scramble through the hinterland.

Destiny seemed against Byron ever reaching Missolonghi. As in Argostoli, so in Dragomestre, he was weather-bound. After sailing on the 3rd, he '*twice*' ran aground on the Scrofes rocks, so that 'the dollars', in his own words, 'had another narrow escape'. The mistico sprang a leak, though admittedly not a serious one. Whereupon a distinctly serio-comic drama was enacted between Byron, Lukas (who had returned on one of the gun-boats) and Dr Bruno. Byron was preparing for a heroic swim ashore carrying the non-swimmer Lukas, when Bruno rushed up shouting, 'Save *him*, indeed! By G-d! save *me* rather . . . !' At the time, Byron's high emotions dissolved in laughter at Bruno. But weeks later he was to remember, in the misery of unrequited love, his willingness to give his life for Lukas:

> *I watched thee on the breakers, when the rock*
> *Received our prow and all was storm and fear,*
> *And bade thee cling to me through every shock;*
> *This arm would be thy barque or breast thy bier.*

9   Missolonghi: 'A Delivering Angel'

Suddenly the sun shone again on Byron's cause, both physically and metaphorically, but with a brightness too extreme to last. He had been held up by further bad weather between two small off-shore islands, where he swam in the January sea to disperse the fleas and lice, acquired after spending days without being able to take off his clothes. But on the night of the 4th they sailed into Missolonghi and anchored. A mistico had brought a Messiah. What a combination. Or in Gamba's words, the people's 'delivering angel' had come.

Next morning Byron performed his expected role. Buttoned into his red uniform (not the second-hand green jacket presented to him by Trelawny, as the latter suggests), he transferred to a picturesque Spetziot boat, with flags, awning and graceful triangular sails, and glided past the Vasilidi fortress and up the lagoon, to the salute of cannon from the Spetziot fleet: in Lega Zambelli's graphic words, quoted by Doris Langley-Moore, a continuous '*rimbombo del cannone*'. The guns of Vasilidi joined in the salute; a change indeed from the welcome which Byron and Hobhouse had received some fourteen years earlier, when the commander of the fort had merely asked to see their passes.

Byron's moment of landing at Missolonghi caught the imagination of all who were present and has been celebrated romantically with brush and pen.

One favourite painting of 1861 shows him standing in the centre of an ecstatic crowd, draped in a white mantle and extending his right hand. The Bishop of Rogon, attended by acolytes with ecclesiastical banners, gives his blessing. Other banners are agitated by Suliot chiefs in their swirling *fustinellas*, while women throw flowers and kneel as if to a saint. One

ABOVE, RIGHT Prince Alexander Mavrocordato, an unusually handsome portrait. RIGHT Byron's landing at Missolonghi, painted in 1861.

fierce-looking Greek propels his young son towards Byron to touch his robe. Behind Byron are his friends Pietro Gamba and Trelawny, the latter in a turban (in fact Trelawny was not there at all, but in the Morea). The reception committee is led by Noto Botsaris, brother of Marco, and by Prince Alexander Mavrocordato.

Byron and Mavrocordato had never set eyes on one another before. They had much in common – though not looks. The prince's sad, wise brown eyes and drooping moustache, his strands of hair falling over a high collar and narrow shoulders, his bow-tie and above all his small, round wire-rimmed spectacles give the impression of a don rather than a man of destiny. But his complete integrity and European culture made him indispensable to the Cause. He and Byron were both aristocrats, both dedicated, both intellectuals fired, perhaps over-inflamed, with military fervour.

Byron went straight to the house reserved for him down on the shore. It no longer stands, but contemporary prints show that it looked Turkish, with projecting balconies, outside staircases, smallish oblong windows and several open turrets, their conical pantile roofs supported by pillars. The ground-

floor was soon to be filled up with Byron's noisy new bodyguard of Suliots, spilling over into the surrounding outhouses, among the horses.

On the first floor, the 'typographical Colonel' planned his newspaper, the *Hellenica Chronica*, with its Utilitarian motto, 'The greatest good of the greatest number'. Byron certainly did not number himself or the Cause among those to whom this unconciliatory 'firebrand' of a publication would do good. The location of the famous printing-press, in a street leading towards the site of Byron's house, is still pointed out today.

Byron covered the walls of his second-floor suite with 'swords, pistols, Turkish sabres, dirks, rifles, guns, blunderbusses, bayonets, helmets, and trumpets', arranged in striking patterns. Thus surrounded with an armoury worthy of the piratical Lambro himself, he could lay his war-plans with the *capitani* and sometimes gaze nostalgically across the foetid lagoon to where the Ionian Islands lay on the dancing sea.

Around this densely populated house lapped many waters. In stormy weather the waves of the salt lagoon in front would meet and mingle with the rainwater ponds and puddles behind. The streets were often canals; but Missolonghi was no Venice of the East. Further behind still, the flat dull fields of the peninsula ran back towards oppressive mountains, whose ominous slate-blue shadows melted into a fantastically moulded ceiling of black and grey cloud. At one moment these clouds were a pendulous threat; at the next, with a flash and a roar, they burst in volleys of rain.

In Byron's day no one had a good word for Missolonghi. Trelawny was to call it 'the most dismal swamp' he had ever seen, 'this mudbank' encircled on three sides by 'shallow slimy sea-waters'. Grudgingly he admitted that this 'morass' would grow rice, this 'crust of a volcano', vines. But all in all it was nothing more than 'a circle of stagnant pools which might be called the belt of death'. It soon would be.

Byron himself foresaw the whole party dying in 'this mud basket' from ague if not the sword, and concluded (with apologies for 'a very bad pun') that it was better to die '*martially* than *marsh-ally*. . . .'

Modern visitors to Missolonghi are not oppressed by such an overwhelming weight of woe and water, especially if they visit the historic peninsula in spring, summer or autumn. Acacias, palms and eucalyptus trees have been planted in the town. The Garden of Heroes, of which more hereafter, is a fresh green retreat. If all its streets are not yet paved and too many of its shop-windows have the glazed stare of Europe's plastic harvest, its central square and Town Hall have character and its cottages outside the town by the lagoon have atmosphere.

In the Town Hall the whole story of the War of Independence is visually told. There are battle-scenes full of heart-break and exact detail; there are maps of old Missolonghi and Western Greece; and there are portraits of the leaders, from Lord Byron to Marco Botsaris, from Prince Mavrocordato to

Spiridion Tricoupi who delivered Byron's funeral oration, from Theodore Colocotrones in his Homeric helmet to Petro Bey who was no more a Bey than Byron. A small museum contains something rarer than these familiar prints: a piece of greyish wood labelled 'The last branch of Byron's Elm, Harrow, July 21st. 1913' – the year when this part of Greece at last became free.

Down by the lagoon, history and a fleeting poignant beauty still exist side by side. This fishy lagoon has attracted so much unflattering attention from past travellers that it begins to sound like the Ancient Mariner's 'rotting sea' filled with 'a thousand thousand slimy things'. But its shallow waters did at least prevent the large Turkish vessels from landing soldiers on the Misso-longhi peninsula itself. They could only stand out to sea maintaining their blockade.

Moreover, between the lagoon and the sea ran what Hobhouse had first described in September 1809 as Missolonghi's 'singular-looking double shore'. When he and Byron spent a night there two months later, they found that the 'double shore' was formed by rows of stakes driven into the sea and, at intervals, wicker huts, between the shallow lagoon (three feet deep) and the open water for several miles. 'Within this fence,' wrote Hobhouse, 'there is a very valuable fishery.' Five miles from the town, the small wooden Fort Vasilidi, also built on piles, examined every boat entering and leaving the lagoon. Here in their sequestered haven the people of Missolonghi had grown prosperous on selling red mullet, caviare and *boutaraga* – roes made into what looked like tiny sausage rolls. The streets were paved and the bazaar was furnished with some 'neat shops'. But Fort Vasilidi and the wicker huts seemed very 'wretched' to Hobhouse on a rainy day, very insecure 'tenements for any animals not amphibious'.

Today a few of the old fishermen's huts still stand on their stilts at the edge of a creek or in the midst of the languid waters. Other cottages on stilts are modern holiday houses for the summer. All together, they form a gentle, rather frozen sequence of picturesque still-life. A modern causeway cuts through the lagoon to the sea-shore. Again there is a deceptive whiff of Venice, as the rows of stout piles rise out of the water on every side. The shores of the lagoon are fringed with feathery green reeds. A strange hard foggy yellow sun sinks into the faintly burnished sea.

There is no doubt that the strong sense of history which pervades Misso-longhi induces sadness: sadness for Byron's death in 1824, followed by the tragic 'Exodus' of the Missolonghiots in 1826. After the terrible siege had become unendurable, the people knelt on the grass to be blessed by the Bishop of Rogon, and then the men rushed forth with their daggers and muskets, to be massacred by the Turks.

Delacroix's painting of *Greece Expiring on the Ruins of Missolonghi* gathers up all the emotional horrors within its frame – or rather, some of the horrors,

for the canvas cannot hold them all. A dead man's hand and arm protrude limply from the right hand corner; the ravished figure of Greece half kneels on a broken slab of marble, half stands on the shattered base of a pillar, while part of a blood-stained corner-stone is thrown down at her feet. Her hands make a wide gesture of despair. Behind, a heap of rubble is cut in two by the frame; a Turkish soldier mounts guard between her and what was once her home.

Missolonghi has since been 'shaken out of its skin' by earthquakes (to quote Napier's phrase), burnt by fire and largely rebuilt. Byron's house was destroyed during World War II. Once there were three arches in the city wall through which soldiers, citizens and animals passed in and out. Now there is only one. Beyond it, the rice fields, vineyards and olive groves are less remarkable than the tall ranks of cypresses, which seem to cut across the landscape in all directions. It is as if they marked the mass graves of those slain in the Exodus.

Only when the plain begins to contract as it enters the valley of the River Evinos, does the atmosphere change and the spell lift. Mountain scenery again takes over, with the lovely river curling between long sweeps of sand and pebbles. Small patches of grass are almost hidden by the bright patchwork of goats and kids. The new, fast road is soon running between splendid cliffs, until it reaches Antirrion, the fort, the efficient ferry and the Gulf.

10 'The Sword, The Banner, and The Field'

There was a ferment of martial excitement in Missolonghi throughout January. Visitors of all kinds crammed the little town, some of them bursting out of the old two-storey Turkish houses built of wood which hung over the narrow streets, others sheltering in tents wherever there was an open space. A horde of Suliots occupied the ex-Pasha's seraglio. Civilians might complain and fear for their property, but the long-haired warriors with fierce moustaches, jangling beads and wolf-skins flying from their shoulders held the place in their grip.

Byron shared the effervescence. He was enchanted by the military project of his new friend Mavrocordato for capturing the important forts on the shores of the Gulf of Patras which were still in Turkish hands: Patras itself and the Castle of the Morea (Rion) on the southern shore and Lepanto on the northern, the latter to be Byron's personal assignment.

Lepanto, like other Greek towns, has changed its name more than once. In the Ancient History books it figures as Naupactus; in medieval times, Lepanto; in Byron's day, Epacto; today, Navpaktos, an attractive place where you can swim and walk with the Gulf of Patras in front, the valley of

Huts on stilts in Missolonghi.

the River Mornos to the east, and the Parnassus range behind. Byron and Hobhouse had seen it across the Gulf in 1809. 'It presents a singular appearance,' wrote Hobhouse, 'being seated on the steep declivity of a hill, and having two walls terminating in a vortex, which is crowned by a castle, commanding the town and harbour.' Hobhouse had heard that the fortress was entirely neglected and used as an enclosure for sheep. This would certainly not have been the case since the Revolution of 1821. Hobhouse continued, 'The fortifications are strengthened by tall walls, which run crossways from one side to the other in parallel lines, and have caused the appearance of the place to be compared to a papal crown. I cannot say the simile struck me; but I read of it in Dr Chandler's travels.'

The town had been first fortified by the Venetians. The battle of Lepanto in 1571 had broken Turkish naval power. Was Byron now to drop the mask of Don Juan of Seville and become another Don John of Austria? A second famous victory at Lepanto might well break Turkish land power in Greece, since Corinth and the Castle of Roumeli were already in Greek hands, and once Lepanto had fallen, Patras and the Castle of the Morea would not long hold out. How strange that these names, which had once meant to Byron nothing but sunshine, oranges and lemons, the Greek classics, busy Turkish seraglios, pistol-shooting for fun and a vista across the blue Gulf, should now stand for military vantage points in a deadly armed struggle.

As a sign of his commitment, Byron took under his command six hundred of the Suliots at Missolonghi, despite his ominous clashes with a smaller number of them in Cephalonia. The Greek government promised to pay one hundred of these unruly patriots, Byron the rest. They were intended to form the nucleus of a Byron Brigade, to which an artillery corps would shortly be attached. When twenty-six hapless Germans arrived on 14 January from the Morea (the remnant of General von Normann's fine body of phillhellenes – and a sad commentary on the fate of idealistic volunteers in foreign wars) Byron took on some of them too. He was spending money as fast as he could get it from his bankers in Italy. As he put it, 'there seems very little specie stirring except mine. . . .'

It would not do for the future Brigadier Lord Byron to lose his youthful vigour and fall too far short of his troops' hardihood. A contemporary print shows him and his 'staff' riding across the Plain of Missolonghi in the midst of his Suliot bodyguard, who trot quite as fast as the horses. To improve his stamina, he rode out in all weathers – and most weathers were vile – and when the fields behind Missolonghi were hopelessly waterlogged, he went by boat to a more solid part of the promontory and there galloped through the olive groves.

On 25 January the good Mavrocordato ceremoniously confirmed in writing His Excellency's appointment as Commander-in-Chief. Byron was formally posted to Lepanto, to beseige it with a force of 3000 men, no less.

He felt his position was strong enough, morally, to give a lead to the Greeks in humanity as well as war. After rescuing a Turkish male prisoner on the 16th, he later did the same for a Turkish woman and her daughter of nine. Byron even hoped to adopt the little Hatadje and send her home as a 'sister' for Ada. Perhaps he saw in this beautiful Turkish child his own imaginary 'Leila' from *Don Juan* come to life. The youthful Juan of the poem does indeed rescue the ten-year-old Turkish girl, Leila. Possibly, also, Byron promised that Hatadje should keep her Moslem faith because he remembered Juan's earlier failure to make a Christian of Leila:

> *But one thing's odd, which here must be inserted*
> *The little Turk refused to be converted.*

Two days after his commission, Byron received important letters from the klepht chief Odysseus in the Morea, suggesting a conference at Salona, the modern Amfissa. If successful, the conference would at last re-unite the hostile Greek factions in the east and west. Lepanto and Salona; on these two names hung the 'delivering angel's' hopes.

And not only his hopes of serving the Cause. Success in the field and in diplomacy with the warlike klephts would lighten Byron's personal burden also. The coming of another birthday on 22 January had recalled to him the many periods of despair into which his passions had plunged him. The list of those he had loved, and who could not give him a lasting love in return, had not been finally closed, even by the mutual love of himself and Teresa Guiccioli. Now *'Beauty'* had struck again in the person of Lukas.

Byron sat down on the eve of his thirty-sixth birthday and arose, probably in the small hours of the 22nd, having written a lament for all his life's un-fulfilled visions, whether human or abstract, and for his fresh enslavement by love's 'chain':

> *The hope, the fear, the jealous care,*
> *The exalted portion of the pain*
> *And power of love, I cannot share,*
> *But wear the chain.*

Suddenly, as at Sounion, his mood changed to contempt, but this time to self-contempt:

> *But 'tis not thus – and 'tis not here –*
> *Such thoughts should shake my soul nor now*
> *Where Glory decks the hero's bier,*
> *Or binds his brow.*

> *The Sword, the Banner, and the Field,*
> *Glory and Greece, around me see!*
> *The Spartan, borne upon his shield*
> *Was not more free.*

The Spartans, according to one tradition, were the ancestors of Byron's Suliots.

It seemed that with Lepanto looming, death on the field was more likely than death in bed. This too Byron accepted, and gladly. 'I take it that a man . . . had better end with a bullet than bark in his body.' Yet it was to be the 'china bark' from the quinine tree which, among other more noxious medicines, was to be his fate at the end.

11 *Lepanto (Navpaktos) : A Dream*

February was to see the crash of all Byron's hopes. Nevertheless, it opened with an affirmation of faith in the 'delivering angel' which eclipsed all that had gone before.

He had been invited to make an appearance at Anatolico. To please the people, he and Gamba dressed themselves in their gaudy best and sailed for three hours north-westwards up the long lagoon to this small town. Anatolico, or Aitolikon today, is planted on an island which divides the greater lagoon of Missolonghi from the inland salt-lake of Anatolico. Two splendid bridges of stone join either end of the island to the Acarnanian mountain ranges in the east and a plain around the mouths of the River Achelous to the west. Hobhouse had described the lagoon as not more than two feet deep. 'Halfway across was the town of Natolico, rising out of the water.' He and Byron had dismissed their horses and passed over in one of the many 'punts' plying to and fro. Neither the Albanian (Turkish) governor nor the English (Greek) vice-consul had been very helpful; but Hobhouse, writing in 1813, still remembered the attentiveness of a Jewish doctor, who told them that 'he was honoured by our partaking of his little misery'.

Things were strikingly different in 1824. Anatolico had been the scene of a Turkish siege the year before, stubbornly and successfully resisted by six hundred patriots and a British naval deserter. When Byron arrived on 1 February 1824, the Anatolicans showed their famous spirit in an exuberant welcome. Their joy, indeed, was so 'unconfined', as the 'Childe' would have put it, and their *feu de joie* of bullets and cannon-balls so abandoned that Byron found himself in danger of becoming the dead Spartan borne home on his shield, as visualised in the birthday poem. Every open gallery and wooden balcony was crowded with women dressed in their long braided cloaks, with embroidered head-scarves and white fichus, waving coloured handkerchiefs and hailing him as 'Saviour of Greece'.

Enough was enough. Byron would not stay longer than one day in this heady atmosphere. Moreover, he knew that the raw materials for his all-important artillery corps were due to arrive any moment from Dragomestre,

The shore at Anatolico.

where they were being unloaded and crated for the passage to Missolonghi in flat-bottomed boats, which would not get stuck in the marsh. After a two-hour rain-swept return journey, Byron was back at his HQ on the evening of the 1st. The soaking they had received was to leave the party in poor health – except for Byron who remained 'very well'. Gamba was struck down with colic and Lukas by a sharp feverish attack. Byron nursed the boy devotedly, later remembering his own anguished feelings in another verse of the last poem:

> *I watched thee when the fever glazed thine eyes,*
> *Yielding my couch and stretched me on the ground,*
> *When overworn with watching, ne'er to rise*
> *From thence if thou an early grave hadst found.*

Byron's wish, here recorded, to die with Lukas rather than live without him, reflected a tragic change in mood. His unhappy last love was holding him more fiercely in thrall than ever, while his early optimism for the Cause was fading.

The precious cargo boats from Dragomestre brought added frustrations, balanced by one positive good.

Deeply irritating was Byron's discovery that the Greeks knocked off work on 4 February because it was a fiesta. Destructive torrents of rain poured down on the beached crates, until Byron himself began rolling them under cover, meanwhile furiously cursing the bigoted Greeks. Later, when the crates were unpacked, Byron heard that an 'elect blacksmith' had brought along 322 Greek testaments, but no coal had been provided by the Committee. Yet coal was essential for a forge capable of manufacturing 'delicacies' like Congreve rockets, as the Peninsular soldiers used to call these much-prized weapons. Hopes of storming Lepanto began to recede.

The arrival, however, on 5 February of the fire-master in charge of the artillery corps brought a rush of human warmth. William Parry was no doubt 'a fine rough subject', in Byron's words. He drank a good deal, bickered tactlessly with Byron's entourage and had none of the graces of an officer and a gentleman. Byron nevertheless valued his all-round competence and was cheered by his salty humour, yarns and quick sympathy. For his part, Parry found Byron exceptionally friendly but pallid and depressed: 'In his heart, he [Byron] felt that he was forlorn and forsaken.' A series of brushes with the 'ungovernable' Suliots (as Parry called them), each one becoming more grave than the last, only served to deepen Byron's anxieties.

The day after Parry's arrival it became evident that no government money existed to pay the 3000 soldiers earmarked for the Lepanto campaign, a large number of whom were not even genuine Suliots. A body of again only six hundred was therefore selected for the Byron Brigade from the thousands trying to pass themselves off as Suliots in order to qualify for dollars.

It had required long argument to get the Suliots out of their barracks in the seraglio which was now needed for Parry's foundry. Before this was fully accomplished, the Suliots retaliated by besieging Byron with demands that the proportion of officers to soldiers in their corps should be drastically raised – in order, as always, to get more dollars. The date was 14 February, but it was to be no St Valentine's Day. As a result of this new pressure on the dollars, Byron's long love affair with the Suliots terminated. 'I will have nothing more to do with the Suliots,' he wrote wrathfully next day; 'They may go to the Turks, or the Devil, – they may cut me into more pieces than they have dissensions among themselves, sooner than change my resolution.'

In his defence it must be recalled that 14 February had brought him two other bad pieces of news, both from the Morea. Colocotrones was planning to march against the constitutionalists; and someone had spread a rumour that Byron was a Turk in disguise, no doubt Byron Pasha or Byron Bey. He

Picture in the house of General Botsaris of Suliot soldiers in Missolonghi with the fortified mountain behind.

could not work off his irritation in outdoor exercise, for it would not stop raining. His rage subsiding as it always did, he was persuaded to re-engage six hundred of the repentant Suliots, if half of them would consent to serve under Noto Botsaris, another member of the heroic Marco's family. But even with this compromise the siege of Lepanto would have to be postponed. The dollars had dealt a cruel blow to his dreams.

That evening Byron had a seizure. Thirsty and harrassed, he had drunk some cider; then, feeling 'a very strange sensation', he stood up, staggered and fell into Parry's arms. His face, wrote Parry in *The Last Days Of Lord Byron*, was much distorted, 'his mouth being drawn to one side'. Yet he was conscious, and it was of Lukas that he thought:

> *And when convulsive throes denied my breath*
> *The faintest utterance to my fading thought,*
> *To thee – to thee – e'en in the gasp of death*
> *My spirit turned, oh! oftener than it ought.*

Still weak though calm next day, Byron was assailed by the two doctors in attendance upon him, Dr Bruno and Dr Julius Millingen, a young English philhellene who had joined him at Metaxata. They applied eight leeches to his forehead. Byron fainted from loss of blood. He had already been dieting rigorously for some weeks, owing to his enforced sedentary life. Now he redoubled the dieting for fear of another fit.

Three days later his last hopes of leading a brigade against Lepanto were destroyed. An 'incident' between a Suliot and a foreign guard outside the foundry resulted in the guard–a Swede named Lieutenant Sass–being killed and the Suliot wounded. Sass had been the best and bravest of the volunteers. The situation was clearly out of hand. A swarm of angry Suliots, on the point of mutiny and mass murder, were restrained only by Byron's prompt order that cannon should be mounted at the gate of his house. It was the 19th. On the 20th, Parry's six foreign mechanics of the artillery corps left in haste for the safety of England: 'They are good men enough,' wrote Byron whimsically, 'but . . . are not used to see shooting and slashing in a domestic quiet way, or (as it forms here) a part of housekeeping'. On the 21st, Colonel Stanhope took himself and his literary equipment off to Athens. With all the mutinous Suliots, except Byron's personal bodyguard, disbanded and sent home, it was good-bye to Lepanto also.

Though Byron made light of the Suliots' dismissal and described to his London agent how he had 'boomed them off', he now had every reason to feel as abandoned and forsaken as Parry had sensed earlier. But still he refused to quit. He liked neither being uprooted nor abandoning the Cause.

Moreover, the omens may have seemed to him somewhat brighter by the end of the month. On the evening after Stanhope's departure there had been what Byron called a 'smart' earthquake, from which everyone escaped unscathed. Byron, weak as he was, may have taken pleasure from the fact that he could none the less protect and comfort the terrified Lukas:

> *The earthquake came, and rocked the quivering wall,*
> *And men and nature reeled as if with wine.*
> *Whom did I seek around the tottering hall?*
> *For thee. Whose safety first provide for? Thine.*

There were various heartening items from England: a picture of Ada at last (he had long pined for one), sent to him by his sister Augusta; good news of *Don Juan's* publication; not to mention a letter from Hobhouse saying that he, Byron, had become a hero in England over night, because of Greece ... The weather was temporarily dry enough for him to ride out on the plain with his bodyguard. And there was always Lyon, his Newfoundland, to bound around him like a Suliot uncorrupted by dollars, and kiss his hand. 'Thou art more faithful than men, Lyon,' Byron would say; 'I trust thee more.'

12 *Salona (Amfissa): A Will o'-the-Wisp*

The good omens, like all hopeful prospects during these last testing months, proved delusive. At Missolonghi the weather deteriorated throughout March. Relentless downpours again cooped up Byron indoors, to chafe at his imprisonment in 'this hole' and to brood over his various ills. If the nightmare scene at Sami was in fact due to a first seizure, he had now had two such attacks. Harrowing fears of a third were not diminished by various alarming symptoms. Palpitations, chest pains, dizziness, sudden flashing lights, irrational feelings of fright, dread of madness, headaches, rages, depression. The wonder was that Byron pursued his goal for Greece with unabated zeal. 'That Greece might still be free' was his unquenchable hope.

> *Yet, Freedom! yet thy banner torn, but flying,*
> *Streams like the thunder-storm against the wind.*

Byron could see plenty of thunder-storms these days, performing this particular feat – like his own faith, flying *against* the currents of opinion and probability.

Another vision had re-emerged early in March to take the place of the lost dream of Lepanto. Young George Finlay, in due course to be the author of an impressive *History of Greece*, arrived from Athens. He had known Byron well in Cephalonia. Now he brought letters from Odysseus, Stanhope and Trelawny urging him to accept that earlier, beguiling proposal of a conference at Salona.

Salona, the modern Amfissa, stands at the head of a valley running up into the mountains of Fokis, where the main road from Lepanto forks right to Delphi before continuing north for Lamia. Byron and Hobhouse had caught a memorable glimpse of Salona on their way to Delphi in 1809. 'We then came suddenly in view of a very romantic prospect,' wrote Hobhouse. 'Before us was a well-cultivated corn plain, bounded by Parnassus, and interspersed with extensive groves of olives; to the right was an opening in the mountains, appearing at first like a chasm, but enlarging by degrees into a valley, through which there ran a small river. Advancing towards Crisso, we had a prospect to the left between the hills of the large town of Salona, the capital of the district, containing two thousand Turkish families. It stands on the brow of a hill, as did Amphissa, the ancient town on whose site it is said to be placed.'

The 2,000 unfortunate Turkish families of Salona had assuredly been wiped out during the Revolution of 1821. But Byron, if he had ever managed to reach Salona in 1824, would have found the remains of enough ancient and medieval walls, fountains and churches to satisfy his limited taste for such delights.

A conference in this historic town among the mountains would have more than one advantage for Byron at a time of increasing strain. Politically, he was prepared to risk much for the unity of Greece, east and west, such as the conference might achieve. The drier air at Salona might restore his shattered health. It was also a chance to link up with 'T' again – Trelawny.

To joke with Trelawny as in the old days would not come amiss. Since the Suliot mutiny and his own illness Byron had been living in acute discomfort. Afraid to eat, taking 'meals' at odd moments and only when the pangs of hunger became insistent, still badgered by endless calls for dollars, dollars, dollars, – though he had expended 59,000 dollars on the Cause since January – Byron seemed to an observer to wish that 'T would return, merely to drive away the people ... and put his house in order.' In short, a meeting with Trelawny and the latter's new associates at Salona was an exhilarating thought compared with the chaos and claustrophobia at Missolonghi.

From mid-March Byron worked on two fronts in a state of determined hope. He and Parry strengthened the defences of Missolonghi against a sweep westwards by the Turks from Larissa; though whether the precipitous sides of Mt Varasova above Missolonghi were really as meticulously fortified by neat spiral walls as contemporary prints suggest, is doubtful. Byron's military enthusiasm increased when a Suliot emissary named Lambro arrived from Theodore Colocotrones. Byron at once proposed to put Lambro in command of a new regular force financed out of his original loan of £4000, as soon as it was repaid to him. Lambro could be regarded as a professional soldier who would impose discipline, since he had served with the English as well as with Marco Botsaris. And was not his name the same as that of Haidée's stern father?

He was the mildest mannered man,
That ever scuttled ship or cut a throat.

On the diplomatic front, Byron was wooed by Mavrocordato as well as Colocotrones. The prince offered him the position of governor-general of all Greece, apart from the Morea and Islands. He decided to cross the River Evinos on 22 March, on his way to Salona and that meeting of minds which would unite Greece. He had seen a swallow on 17 March – and gaily told Teresa so.

13 'Glory and Greece'

One swallow did not make a spring in Missolonghi. Indeed, March went out in curtains of rain. The River Evinos was in spate and every field and road in that wide plain under water. Byron's journey to Salona had to be postponed. Did this mean that his last chance to get away from Missolonghi and find life and health elsewhere had vanished? Perhaps it did. Byron's detention at Missolonghi may, on the contrary, have preserved his freedom and even life for another few weeks. He heard of a plot to kill Prince Mavrocordato and kidnap himself at Salona, where he would then be held to ransom. The stupendous loan raised by the London Committee, of which he would be the administrator, was known to be coming from England. Such a loan held out every inducement to fraud and force.

The dual blow of Lepanto and Salona to Byron's spirit could not be concealed. William Parry spoke of his 'lost enthusiasm' followed by peevishness and gloom. 'A mist fell from Lord Byron's eyes. He owned that his sagacity was at fault, and he abandoned all hope of being able to guide the Greeks. . . . He feared that the proceeds of a loan might be misspent by one party . . . many honest families [idealistic subscribers to the loan] might lose their money by Philhellenism.' Byron loved the Cause strongly: was it wrongly also?

William Parry made a mistake in implying that the scales had only now fallen from the poet's eyes. The subtler Finlay had long ago noticed that his friend possessed something of a split personality: part decisive male of cool clear judgment, part sympathetic woman easily moved and managed. Byron's clear-eyed, rational approach to the Greek cause had always coexisted with his romantic feelings. His present disillusionment was due to the onrush of almost insuperable difficulties. The coming of the loan would pose a new problem of incredible delicacy: how to distribute so much gold without actually financing civil war. Even the man in Byron quailed, as any man might. Quailed, but did not quit. What he had written before the Salona plan crashed still held good. 'I cannot quit Greece while there is a chance of my being of any (even supposed) utility; there is a stake worth millions such as I am, and while I can stand at all I must stand by the cause.' Or in his earlier, equally prophetic words, 'I must see this Greek business out (or it *me*). . . .'

At the same time, another side of his masculinity was bitterly disappointed. He poured into the last verse of his last poem all his wounded love for Greece and for the Greek boy Lukas:

> *Thus much and more; and yet thou lov'st me not,*
> *And never will! Love dwells not in our will.*
> *Nor can I blame thee, though it be my lot*
> *To strongly, wrongly, vainly love thee still.*

Nevertheless, these last weeks were not all misery. Byron could still plan ahead. If there were another miracle of St Dionysius, as in January, and he led the Byron Brigade to the liberation of Lepanto, new vistas of service would open out. Accredited to a Greek central government, he would sail to the United States and persuade 'that free and enlightened govern-ment' to set the example of recognising the Federation of Greece as an 'independent state'.

Sometimes, however, federation, even normal friendliness among Greeks, seemed further away than ever. At the beginning of April a fierce quarrel broke out between a band of Anatolicans under a chieftain named George Karaiskakis, and the citizens of Missolonghi. Fifty-six Anatolican rebels captured the fort of Vasilidi, two Missolonghian primates were taken as hostages and Karaiskakis was rumoured to have sold these neighbours of his to the Turkish fleet. It was only Byron's spirited deployment of gun-boats which forced the rebels to retire from Vasilidi.

During this fracas the skies over Missolonghi cleared at last and Byron and his bodyguard boldly took a six-mile ride outside the walls. Having tasted freedom, he refused to stay indoors when the rain clouds closed in again. On Friday, 9 April, he and Pietro Gamba got wet through with rain and perspiration after a stiff gallop and then spent half an hour being rowed home in an open boat. That evening Byron shuddered with feverish pains. 'I do not care for death,' he groaned to Gamba, 'but these agonies I cannot bear.' Next day, though still feverish, he mounted his horse again, Lambro leading the cavalcade. As he rode through the wet olives Byron remembered the words of a Scottish soothsayer in his youth: 'Beware your thirty-seventh year.' Dr Bruno was sent for that night. His art was not greatly superior to the fortune-teller's.

On Sunday morning, after a hot bath and castor oil, Byron was advised by Bruno to be bled. When he refused, as he had always refused such treatment, Bruno substituted for the bleeding six doses of antimony powders. Parry, filled with alarm, prepared to remove the patient to Zante where greater professional skills were available. He had found that Byron's mind was

The lagoon at Missolonghi.

wandering. Monday's treatment was a repeat of Sunday's. Byron had again refused bleeding either by the knife or leeches. Tuesday should have been the day on which he sailed to Zante; but as before when he had planned to leave Missolonghi, the weather deteriorated, a sirocco blew up and he could not go. Byron's medical attention deteriorated also, in the sense that Dr Julius Millingen, the young Englishman, was called in as a consultant, and added his weight to Bruno's opinion that the patient must be bled – in the end.

However, Byron still resisted with the support of Parry. So there was another large dose of castor oil followed by higher fever and stomach ache, with Epsom salts and a foot-bath to relieve the pain. Byron slept badly that night. Next morning, Wednesday the 14th, he got up as usual and between bouts of delirium demanded his horse or boat. Back in bed, he recited and construed Latin hexameters from his schooldays, to make sure his mind was not failing. Again Bruno and Millingen tried to persuade him to be bled. Byron's mind was still clear enough to retort that 'the lancet had killed more people than the lance.' Thursday was the same; the doctors pressing for bleeding, Parry encouraging Byron's opposition. 'I have had several inflammatory fevers during my life ... when I was much more robust and plethoric than I am now,' said Byron; 'yet I got through them without bleeding. This time, also I will take my chance.' The doctors fell back on the only other treatment they knew of, dosing.

During the seventh night of his illness he was attacked by a spasmodic cough. At once Dr Bruno pounced. Only bleeding, he said, would prevent the cough from developing into pneumonia. At this Byron promised to be bled next day; but when Friday morning arrived his spirits returned after a better sleep than he had expected, and the lancet was declined yet again. Fate then guided Dr Millingen to a more effective appeal even than the one made by Dr Bruno the night before. If Byron was nervous about his lungs, he positively dreaded the loss of his reason. When Millingen spoke of Byron's risking, not his life, but his cerebral system, the sick man capitulated. 'Come; you are, I see, a d——d set of butchers. Take away as much blood as you will; but have done with it.'

Then began the awful tale of these unwitting Shylocks, measuring his blood pound by pound in their medical containers and meanwhile pre-scribing massive doses of purgatives. Byron's delirious raving about death in English and Italian so much frightened Dr Bruno that he had his pistols removed from the bedside. No doubt Dr Millingen was glad that Augusta's bible remained. He had been shocked to hear the 'irreligious' Byron say, 'Shall I sue for mercy? Come, come, no weakness! let's be a man to the last.'

The last day of consciousness came for Byron on Easter Sunday. Four doctors were by now round his bedside and, scarcely more ominously, twelve leeches. When applied to his temples they drew two more pounds of blood. The 'bark' or quinine which Byron had once feared more than death from a bullet was duly administered. But he had the consolation of imagining, at least, that the bullets were flying round his head. 'Forwards – forwards – courage,' he shouted, '– follow my example – don't be afraid.' No one ever needed to say that to *him* in real life. His courage was invincible.

As he slowly sank surrounded by weeping servants and distraught doctors who had realised his danger too late, his thoughts turned with pity towards all those whom he felt he had failed: his wife, his child Ada, his 'poor sister', his 'poor servants', the 'poor town' – 'Poor Greece'.

Greece was 'poor' not because of any failure on his part but despite all his sacrifices. Long ago he had spoken with whimsical self-pity of 'poor B'. Now self was forgotten in the fate of Greece. 'My wealth, my abilities, I devoted to her cause,' he said to Millingen on his death-bed. '... Well: there is my life to her.'

The people of Missolonghi knew it was true. Though the day was Easter Sunday, there were no festive hymns or songs to be heard near his house, and for once no trigger-happy Greeks letting off their pistols in the crowded rooms on the ground floor. They kept silence, of all things the most difficult for them.

'Now I want to sleep,' he murmured at six o'clock on the Sunday evening. He died without waking again on Easter Monday, 19 April 1824, at the same hour.

14   *Crede Byron : Epitaph for a Hero*

'Here let my bones moulder,' the dying poet said. 'Lay me in the first corner without pomp or nonsense.'

It was a strange request to come from a man whose name echoed from end to end of Europe, with the long roll of the romantic credo; and as the end drew nearer still, Byron expressed a wish for England. He was given Christian burial in Hucknall Torkard church near Newstead. His belief in an after life had been charmingly expressed to Parry at Missolonghi: 'Eternity and space are before me; but on this subject, thank God, I am happy and at ease. The thought of living eternally, of again reviving, is a great pleasure.' His lungs were buried in St Spiridion's church at Missolonghi.

Meanwhile the 'poor Greece' of his last thoughts went into mourning, fired her 37 minute guns for his thirty-seventh year – and reaped the fruits of a sacrifice which he had sadly expected to be barren. The fall of Missolonghi in 1826 would have been just one more 'horror of war' except for Byron's having given his life two years before. Because of this, the tragedy of 1826 shocked Europe. But for Byron's death, the Turkish fleet might have been left untouched at Navarino Bay in 1827, to extinguish the last flames of Greek freedom. Instead, fifty-seven of its warships were sunk by twenty-six British, French and Russians.

Throughout the rest of the century Greece slowly gathered herself together as a nation. Byron's tireless preaching against faction and his faith in Greek unity may have seemed to founder during his lifetime; his death gave them immediate and impressive credibility. If Lord Byron, the most famous figure in Europe, had chosen to link his name with strife-torn, down-trodden, 'poor Greece', hers must indeed be a cause worth fighting for.

The city of Athens has selected a striking site for her monument to Byron. It stands at the corner of the Zappeion Gardens in direct line with the Parthenon, where Byron lamented the lost marbles, and the Monument of Lysikrates, where he wrote poetry and hummed Romaic love-songs. Heavy traffic hums today around the naturalistic figures of the Byron Monument, grouped high on their cylindrical pediment. Hellas crowns the hero-poet with laurels. The pair of French nineteenth-century sculptors are a good deal further from the spirit of the Parthenon than the statue's physical distance might suggest; but dazzlingly white pentelic marble seen against a blue Greek sky is a sufficiently beautiful thing in itself for one to accept this sensuous, romantic representation of 'Childe Harold', in place of the indomitable figure who came to Greece for the last time.

To walk across to Missolonghi's Garden of Heroes which lies beside the city 'Gate of the Exodus', is to discover an oasis of shady green palms, cypresses and pines under a scorching sun, and of raised or sunken vistas in a flat land. The garden has a touching charm. It is in fact a public park dedicated to all Missolonghi's heroes of the War of Independence. A mound in the centre is the burial place of unknown soldiers. On the right is a recumbent statue to Marco Botsaris, reminiscent of the classical dying Gaul. Would it be churlish to wish that the sculptor had allowed him his Suliot capote? Between the tumulus and the Botsaris statue stands a tall marble figure of Byron, high up on a double plinth. He wears the same dress as on his pedestal in Athens, civilian coat and trousers with a loose collar, flowing neck-tie and a classical mantle. But above his coat of arms is a royal crown; perhaps a sign that he was to have been offered the sovereignty of Greece at Salona, and certainly that the Greeks regarded him as a king among men.

Hidden under the trees and statuary are the small kiosks of photographers, where visitors to the *Heroon*, as the Garden of Heroes is called, can be photographed beside their favourite freedom fighter.

There is a promise that another memorial to Byron will be erected at Missolonghi, in the square between his garden and the Hotel Liberty. This will be a Centre for Liberal Studies, built on the site of the house where he spent the four most arduous, anxious and, in a practical sense, fruitful months of his life.

Crede Byron – Trust Byron – is the family motto. There had been a time when it seemed a mockery; when Caroline Lamb, who considered herself betrayed, fitted out her pages with buttons bearing the motto, *Ne Crede Byron*. To the Establishment he was at best a libertine at worst satanic. Never a man to trust. Even Byron sometimes feared his own impact: unhappy himself, he felt that he blighted those nearest to him.

His last months in Greece dispelled all such thoughts. *Crede Byron* became his motto in deeds as in words. The people trusted him. Where others were greedy, corrupt or faint-hearted, he gave all, took nothing and never faltered.

The nineteenth-century statue of Byron at the corner of the Zappeion Gardens in Athens.

177

The Greek poet Solomos, whose island home of Zante Byron had briefly visited on his way to Missolonghi, and where they may well have met, lamented his death in a long lyric. After Missolonghi itself fell, Solomos mourned over it in his most famous poem, *The Free Besieged*. Here he suddenly saw beauty and terror united in pure light –

Light that tramples smiling Hell and death.

Mystical though this light be, it has a share in the luminosity which permeates every rock and wave of Byron's Greece. It is the light which gives life to Byron's death.

'I am ashes,' wrote Byron, 'where once I was fire.' This image haunted him.

Glory, like the phoenix 'midst her fires,
Exhales her odours, blazes, and expires.

But glory and Greece, like the phoenix, rise again. And with them is the name of Byron.

ACKNOWLEDGMENTS

All the photographs in this book were taken by Jorge Lewinski other than those
mentioned below. Mr Lewinski is grateful to General Botsaris for permission to take
the photographs on pages 146–7 at his library.

The author and publishers are grateful to the following for permission to reproduce
pictures: on page 9, by gracious permission of H.M. The Queen; pages 90 and 114,
The British Library; page 113, National Portrait Gallery; pages 11 and 119,
Newstead Abbey Collections.

Many quotations in this book are taken by kind permission of John Murray Limited
from *Letters of Byron (A Self Portrait)* by Peter Quennell and *Byron–a Life* by
Leslie A. Marchand.

The verse quoted in this book comes from *Byron's Works Complete in One Volume*
published by John Murray (London 1837).

The maps on pages 22–3 were drawn by Edward McAndrew Purcell.

BIBLIOGRAPHY

A short Bibliography of Byron's life in addition to his collected Poetical Works.

Byron's Verse – A choice of, Selected with an introduction by Douglas Dunn (paperback) 1974.

Byron : Selected Prose Edited with introduction by Peter Gunn (paperback) 1972.

Byron's Letters and Journals There are many collections of which the most recent and comprehensive (but still in process of being edited and published) is by Professor Leslie A. Marchand, vols. I–III, 1798–1814. 1973–4.

Elwin, Malcolm: *Lord Byron's Wife,* 1962.

Finlay, George: *A History of Greece,* vols 6–7
The Greek Revolution, 1877.

Gamba, Count Peter: *A Narrative of Lord Byron's Last Journey to Greece,* 1825

Grylls, R. Glynn: *Claire Clairmont, Mother of Byron's Allegra,* 1939;
Trelawny, 1950.

Hobhouse, John Cam: *A Journey through Albania . . .,* 1813.

Hunt, Leigh: *Lord Byron and Some of his Contemporaries,* 1828.

Jenkins, Elizabeth: *Lady Caroline Lamb,* (paperback) 1972.

Leake, William Martin: *Travels in Northern Greece,* vol. 4, 1820.

Lovelace, Ralph Milbanke, Earl of: *Astarte, A Fragment of the Truth concerning George Gordon, Sixth Lord Byron,* 1905, reprinted 1921.

Marchand, Leslie A.: *Byron – A Portrait,* 1971
A Biography, 3 vols., 1957.

Medwin, Thomas: *Conversations of Lord Byron . . . at Pisa,* 1824.

Moore, Doris Langley: *The Late Lord Byron,* 1961
Lord Byron – Accounts Rendered, 1974.

Moore, Thomas: *Leters & Journals of Lord Byron, with . . . Life,* 1830.

Millingen, Julius: *Memoirs of the Affairs of Greece,* 1831.

Napier, Priscilla: *Revolution and The Napier Brothers,* 1973.

Nicolson, Harold: *Byron – The Last Journey,* 1934.

Origo, Iris: *The Last Attachment,* 1949
Allegra, 1935.

Parry, William: *The Last Days of Lord Byron,* 1825.

Polidori, John William: *The Diary,* edited by W.M. Rosetti, 1911.

Quennell, Peter: *Byron The Years of Fame – Byron in Italy,* 1974 (republished).

St Clair, William: *That Greece Might Still Be Free – The Philhellenes in the War of Independence,* 1972.

Strickland, Margot: *The Byron Women,* 1974.

Trelawny, Edward John: *Records of Shelley, Byron and the Author,* 1858, (paperback, 1973).

INDEX